The Creator of the Universe

The Creator of the Universe

From Polarity to a Better World

A. Curiel

Kindle Publishing Package

Copyright © A. Curiel, 2015

All rights reserved. No part of this book may be reproduced in any form without permission in writing from the author. Reviewers may quote brief passages in reviews.

ISBN-13: 978-0692939406

ISBN-10: 0692939407

DISCLAIMER

No part of this publication may be reproduced or transmitted in any form or by any means, mechanical or electronic, including photocopying or recording, or by any information storage and retrieval system, or transmitted by email without permission in writing from the author.

Neither the author nor the publisher assumes any responsibility for errors, omissions, or contrary interpretations of the subject matter herein. Any perceived slight of any individual or organization is purely unintentional.

Any resemblance, within this book, to real persons living or dead is purely coincidental apart from my own stories that are true to the author.

Cover Design: A. Curiel

Translation: Pamela Rodriguez

Editing: Jessica Beeson

Photos: A. Curiel & Alessandra Rodriguez

Dedication

We all would like to live a balanced life, however, for the most part we all swing from one polarity to another. Polarity is present in every aspect of life. There is a light side and a dark side; nevertheless, as we ascend, we will bring our self-awareness into oneness. Only then will we begin to integrate the light and the dark into unity, with one source of energy from which all things originate: love.

The longer you explore one polarity, the further you stray from achieving the ideal balance. Accentuating the polarity actually adds to the polarity of any given circumstances. Within the book, you will find tools on how to manage your polarity in a more effective manner, allowing you to make the best out of any situation.

May the light be with you always.

Contents

1. The Creator 1
2. The Creation of New Worlds 18
3. The Intervention of the Gods 31
4. Brahman Journeys to Tellus 42
5. Mester's Lessons 55
6. The Threat of King Aldon 101
7. The Journey to Moorea 109
8. The Intervention of the Gods............................ 124
9. The Dragon Belt 126
10. The Secret of Moorea 134
11. The Creator Looses Patience 161
12. The Return to Tallen 164
13. The Welcoming of Brahman 196

1

The Creator

It all began with an enormous, effervescent reaction as if an Alka-Seltzer had fallen into the bottomless cup of the universe. An incandescent light took over as gasses escaped, devouring the void with great pleasure. That place, once as dark as the minds of the most wicked beings, was finally being brought into the light.

Trends in the entropy of the universe manifested freely, and the arbitrary movements of the gases multiplied at great speed. Not a single space in the cosmos remained empty. Matter rose in temperature and pressure, intensifying in preparation of a massive explosion. However, an opposite reaction followed. With the fizzing effect now losing momentum, the gasses dissipated while being drawn into a black hole. Resembling a huge hungry mouth, every piece of remaining matter swallowed up into the unknown.

The emptiness now had a new stage with a golden light enveloping the black hole as witness to a luminous embryo formation. Covered with a thin layer of translucent skin, it revealed how the millions of atoms arranged themselves as if knowing exactly what to do. Inside the embryo, it was fluidic and lukewarm. Slowly, the heat began progressively increasing, causing a strong chemical bond between the atoms to form thirteen undivided molecules. The universe became a womb for this new growth, nourishing it as its baby.

The subtle curves of the embryo gradually started forming the outline of its features. It had no hair, but its most striking feature were two massive globular eyes, missing each other by millimeters. Each eye was composed of millions of multifaceted receptors, giving it a 360-degree visual field.

The Creator of the Universe

Its silvery smooth, spade shaped beard gave him an air of solemnity. Like a Lord, with an upright posture, it revealed how the center of its body was formed by a column of energetic waves, flowing toward its head while projecting images of light.

When he opened his eyes, they were so big that the entire universe awoke with them. He discovered the infinite present, but that was all he knew. His existence revolved around the unchangeable and omnipresent void. Everything remained the same. The deafening silence took root in his deepest of thoughts and the unknown began to consume him. *Who am I? What am I doing here? Where did I come from?*

Something was missing. Loneliness began to take a toll on him. With a long sigh, all his receptors closed simultaneously, leaving his thoughts to fixate on one idea: *companionship.*

When he opened his eyes, two brilliant spheres of equal size appeared on each of his palms. His lips curved into his first smile. The spheres were warm and malleable. Overcome with fascination, he exercised his hands in a playful manner, wondering what to do next. Instinctively, he brought them together and overlapped them until they met at their midpoints. Acting as its trigger, a beaming white light shot out, forcing him to blink several times. His gaze was as still as if each eye had a million pins stuck on it.

Atoms multiplied faster than his eyes could follow. This time, arranging themselves into seven undivided molecules. He was in such awe that he had to remind himself to blink. He somehow knew something had ended—or was it just beginning?

A foreign figure emerged from the light. It was about three-fourths his own height and leaner than himself. It had a long beard and hair that appeared to be one continuous unit. A gray cloak was covering his body from head to toe,

The Creator of the Universe

and even though he had most of his face covered, his penetrating icy blue eyes did not escape the Creator's attention. His gestures reflected a great sense of serenity, and his smile framed the portrait of humility.

The Creator of the Universe

With his head down, he bent onto his knees and said, "I am Brahman, My Creator."

The Creator approached him and lifted him up by the arms to hug him chest to chest. He wanted to reassure himself that this was real. Their proximity vacuumed any feeling of loneliness he may have had within seconds.

"Wait", he thought, "Did you say, 'My Creator'?" Every single one of his millions of receptors looped around in search of answers as he tried to understand this man's choice of words.

His eyes lingered on Brahman. *Now, I understand. My own thoughts gave him life, so the universe is just a great idea.* The Creator could see so deeply into this man's mind that it brought tears to his eyes. He fully perceived this new being's every emotion as his own. His face lit up as he realized that he was responsible for such a beautiful creation.

As time passed, the Creator's need to create grew exponentially. Even though Brahman filled his heart with more joy than he could have ever hoped for, his creative instinct would not allow him to rest. His receptors closed again as it came time for the next creation. With no limits to stop him, he imagined he was the architect whose hands held the universe.

In a thunder of fingers, the universe became a gallery full of masterpieces. Mass, energy, and space gave rise to constellations, galaxies, and black holes. The universe grew like a massive city under construction.

With his eyes fixed and unwavering, Brahman looked around. It seemed like a great scene with new actors added into the script.

"I wish I could help," Brahman thought, witnessing every move with awe.

The Creator smiled and looked at him with a sly look as his eyes closed again for the next creation.

The Creator of the Universe

Brahman knew that something was about to take form as his eyes spun in search of any slight changes, but they were unable to find anything new.

"The new is within you Brahman. I gave you the gift of geometry. Go on, try." The Creator smiled this time.

A spark of light pierced Brahman's mind, it was as if he had lit an imaging machine. Different surfaces and volumes appeared creating complex geometric figures.

Their thoughts intertwined with such accuracy that there was no interference of any kind. The creation of one complemented the other. Their ideas were threaded within a blanket of universal love.

Brahman stopped for a moment, and crossed his eyebrows, letting his thoughts roam.

"My Creator, if you would allow me to ask, you have created this beautiful universe, and given me an extraordinary gift, but why is it just you and me?"

"I'm afraid I don't understand your question, Brahman," said the Creator with confusion.

"If you had the ability to create me, why not create others?"

"Eh..." The Creator paused for a moment, "I suppose I haven't thought about it. Your presence is so fulfilling that I haven't had the need to create any more beings."

Brahman's question made him realize that he had a great responsibility as a Creator, as well as of the infinite number of possibilities open to him just waiting for a single thought.

Without letting another moment pass, he let his imagination run free. He closed his eyes with great enthusiasm and said, "Here are my new creations."

This time, the Creator felt an even greater responsibility because lives were now involved. Even though he gave life to Brahman, it was an unconscious creation, since he was unaware of his powers. This time, it was different. The muscles of his jaw began to tighten as he tried to coordinate the millions of receptors to remain closed for a moment, which was no easy task. After a few seconds, he slowly opened his eyes. This time, ten spheres of equal size appeared around him, positioning themselves as if marking time in a ten-hour based clock. The spheres looked very similar to the ones he used with Brahman, except for two of them whose light was significantly dimmer, almost opaque in their texture. He took the first four pairs of luminous spheres and intersected them. He then turned to the other two spheres unsure of what to do. *Why doubt this now if it is only two spheres*? Bringing his hands together in front of his chest, he started tapping his fingers for an answer. It was as if his intuition was trying to warn him.

    The first four creations had already begun to develop, increasing the intensity of their light as they grew. With clouds of doubt, the Creator grabbed the last two spheres with trembling hands as he finally intersected them.

    This was something Brahman had never seen before. The Creator seemed indecisive. In his heart, he wanted to intervene, but his respect for the Creator was stronger than the hesitation he saw in him.

    They stepped back with especially alert eyes. Of the five creations, four followed the same pattern as Brahman. However, the fifth creation was different. The atoms formed a mere three molecules when it stopped the process of growth. Only half of the creation projected light, while the other half remained dark and muddy.

    Brahman was noting the worry on his Creator's face as he observed the fifth creation. Even when he did not understand the process of creation well, he did not need any knowledge to understand that something was not right.

    BOOOOMM! An explosion rang the bell of the first creation.

    Between a burst of stars, two enormous white wings released, fluttering free as it took flight. The undulating feathers moving freely like paintbrushes, uncovered infinite shades of colors. His muscular body was imposing, accompanied by a slender, thick neck with an elegant head.

The Creator of the Universe

Projecting a magical appearance, glimmers of moon dust completely covered his body, shining like stars upon him.

The Creator of the Universe

The connection between colors and emotions was profound in this being, increasing the vividness of his surroundings.

Landing on four legs with a well-developed sense of balance, he approached the Creator.

"Who are you?" asked the Creator in amazement as his eyes reflected every pigment of color on this creature.

"My name is Celare, and I am the God of Wisdom." He bent his front right hoof as he tilted his head as a sign of respect.

"Welcome, my beloved Celare. What a joy it is to have you with us."

Tannn......! A very unusual noise interrupted them. It was a connection between music and emotions. The intuitive link to the sound made the Gods go into a dance. It was melodic and very contagious, causing their moods to become jubilant.

"My Creator, someone else is approaching us," Brahman quietly interrupted, fighting the urge to dance himself.

As the new creation moved closer, they noticed a body about a quarter of the size of the Creator. His eyes were large and tilted upward, and his cheeks were pushed up into two red lumps by a wide smile. The curly haired boy could not hide his two large, pointy ears that behaved somewhat like satellites, capturing the slightest of sounds.

He wore a black-tailed coat like a well-dressed conductor, making him look very formal even though his movements and appearance were childish.

Walking in a perfectly orchestrated manner, he approached the Creator and said, "I am Kozma, the God of Music."

The Creator of the Universe

    The Creator smiled widely as he embraced Kozma, feeling protective of his new childlike creation. "Thank you Kozma. Your gift is very welcome."

    Unexpectedly, their bodies were wet with one blow. The Creator's eyes filled with water, giving the appearance that he was at the brink of tears.

    They quickly turned to face the culprit of such an act. A more stylized figure was completely covered by a drizzle of water that clothed her. Her blue hair grew steadily, like the springs of a river. She had two green eyes, the kind of green that pushes through snow to remind you that spring is coming. In the middle of her forehead, held by a golden tiara, she had a precious oval stone which changed colors based on her emotions. A single glance from this being pierced the soul by taking possession of the spirit.

As she turned towards the Creator, her deep gratitude caused the stone on her forehead to shift into the color of a deep ocean.

"I apologize for the short notice. I am Astra, and I am the God of the Fountain of Life." She could see in their faces the unexpected reaction to her appearance.

The Creator wiped his face and introduced her to the others. Having her close to him was a completely different sensation; one of being constantly drenched was something he would have to get used to around her.

Celare jumped, fluttering around Astra without rest, until he fell face-up at her mercy, twisting from side to side struggling to get back up to his feet. He felt an unexplainable pleasure from the drizzle in her presence.

"Well, I think someone's going to be staying a lot cleaner!" Kozma muttered between his teeth, while his shoulders curled with laughter.

With great force, the springs from Astra's hair began to shift in a different direction. It felt like a large vacuum cleaner was absorbing everything in its path. Celare tried to resist this force as he covered Astra with his wings. Kozma clung tightly to the Creator's hand while Brahman paralyzed, only his sweetened eyes giving any signs of life. His impression of the new creation was stronger than the fear of her force.

From afar, white hair fluttered, dazzling the creations and a stylized silhouette figure drew closer, dragging a long silver dress and marking an air of royalty. In affirmation, a crown adorned in diamonds illuminated her face, highlighting her honey-colored eyes, capable of commanding anyone who stared into them.

She carried with great pride a pregnant belly, lighting up as a full moon with an exquisite beauty that baffled them all. Her presence created an urgent need in those around her to know more about this mystical being.

The Creator of the Universe

The Creator of the Universe

With supreme elegancy, she placed her hands on her belly and bent her knees half way, "I am Losna, the God of Magnetism."

The color on Brahman's face began to ignite, barely able to disguise the redness between his mustache and beard. Attempting to hide it further, he moved his cloak more onto his face, making him look even more timid.

The Creator immediately realized what was happening and quickly changed the subject by introducing her to the rest.

Before the Creator could say another word, he lost his balance as he felt a strong pull from behind. Kozma was trembling uncontrollably, holding on tight to one of the Creator's legs, glancing between pieces of cloth as the last creation approached them.

With everything happening, the Creator had forgotten about the incident that had worried him so much.

A corpulent man with firmly planted feet and his chin high up in the air stared down at them. Strangely, his body gave the impression of being divided into two. His left side emitted light and was the living expression of kindness with hair so white that it could even make snow look gray. In contrast, his right side was very dark. His greasy black hair, framed a wicked eye, and a widely curved mouth gave the impression of perverse satisfaction. Depending on the angle from which they observed, he could be seen as two completely different people.

"My name is YinYang, and I am the God of Polarity." His tone could not have been more arrogant.

The sound of the springs stopped, while Kozma played a note of terror, Taratatannnn... Not a single creation moved, incapable of hiding the bewilderment on their faces. The Creator sensed something different in YinYang, but could not quite put his finger on it. However, in the hopes of

The Creator of the Universe

treating all his creations equally, he introduced him to the others.

The Creator of the Universe

The universe became a different place now through the graceful notes heard in Kozma's melodies and the colors of Celare's wings. Astra refreshed them with her showers, and Losna's magnetic attraction constantly shifted with her mood. The only element who constantly clashed was YinYang, who was incapable of successfully completing any creation because his forces were always at odds. There was an equal and opposite reaction to everything he did. His only accomplishment was an odd structure that floated atop his head at all times.

The Creator of the Universe

The Creator was delighted with his new creations, but he frequently pondered why YinYang's creation had been so different from the others.

"What is that element constantly floating above your head?" the Creator asked YinYang.

"Oh! Do you like it?" YinYang exclaimed, excited to have finally caught his attention. "It's a balance to reach equilibrium between polar opposites—a middle point," YinYang answered confidently.

Despite having given life to him, the Creator could not understand YinYang at all.

"Polar opposites?" the Creator questioned with his mind at a crossroads.

"Let me explain, my Creator. When you observe my left side, you see light, which I suspect is your more preferred side."

"Tan!" An interruption came from Kozma.

"When you see my right, I am much darker, hard to see and even to accept. But, when you see me from the front, you're capable of seeing both of my sides, thereby understanding me better."

The Creator nodded slightly, indicating that he understood, but he could not help but wonder what the point of it all was. He had already noticed that consciously or not, the rest of the gods always positioned themselves on YinYang's left, except for Kozma, whose high sense of perception made him feel uncomfortable regardless of which side he was. The Creator was the only one who positioned himself in front of YinYang, in the hopes of understanding him better. After all, he had created him.

2
The Creation of New Worlds

There comes a point in all schooling when the teacher must trust that they have provided their students with the necessary foundation to grow and continue to build on the knowledge they have been given.

"As your Creator, I have a great responsibility to the universe, which is why I will be assigning each of you a creation. Of course, you all have free will and can accept or reject to take part. I will allow each of you to form a creation with no interference from me. The only rule will be that no creation can interfere with another creation of higher frequency. For this reason, every creation will be placed in a different dimension according to its frequency or evolutionary level," he explained.

Kozma danced to the front, trumpeting a melody, "On your mark, get set, go!" The Creator laughed, his spontaneity was always catching them by surprise. Brahman, Celare, Astra, and Losna also moved forward, taking glimpses of YinYang, who hung back. He knew he was different and not entirely accepted, and he feared that his creation would not be accepted either. As expected, his dark-egotistical side would not allow him to fall back for too long, so he finally stepped forward with his head held high.

The Creator continued, "I will create twelve spheres, giving each of you two of them. Brahman is familiar with this process, seeing that he was with me throughout all of your creations. You will move your two spheres toward each other until their midpoints intersect. It is crucial; however, that prior to this, you envision what your new creation will be. Take your time and imagine every single detail. I will not interfere, but you will be able to help one another if you wish. The only thing you will not be allowed to alter is the dimension in which your creation is placed in order to avoid interference among them. If a change in dimension or evolutionary level is to occur, it must come from within. Remember the great responsibility you owe to your creations and to the universe."

"What are dimensions?" Losna asked.

"Dimensions are the level of freedom with which we can experiment in space. The higher the dimension, the greater the freedom. In this way, creations in lower dimensions will be restricted in their use of space, which will prevent them from affecting other creations in their journey toward knowledge."

"This seems fair," YinYang said. "So you mean to say that the creation that achieves the highest dimension will be the winner?"

All the receptors in the eye of the creator opened simultaneously trying to understand such a comment. "There is no winner or loser; there is only unity. We are all one, which is why I am allowing you to help each other." YinYang was full of surprises—and not necessarily good ones.

"This is simply an exercise to see how you all work together as a team." The Creator could not hide his concern about YinYang's question.

"If there are no further questions, you may proceed to pick up your spheres. I wholeheartedly trust each and every one of you," the Creator looked specifically at YinYang with an inquisitive look.

Again, Kozma was the first to move forward, his curiosity was constantly getting the better of him. With much security, he took the spheres. This time he did not look like a child, his index fingers shot out and his torso moved back and forth, directing his ears like a baton. The music poured forth—precisely coordinated and emotionally expressive.

In response to this sublime podium dance, his new creation took form. Planet Muza appeared in the Nuzair galaxy. Fine sand covered the surface, so light that it could float. The whole planet had millions of organ pipes in different sizes intersected from its center. In the heart of the planet, he placed the Grand Organ of Krasis, capable of producing 144,444 different musical notes.

With every vibration over the surface it caused the sand shifted, dividing into regions forming different patterns and consequently the new inhabitants, The Cladnis. These beings could perceive and retain all vibrations within themselves, allowing them to fully understand the concept of sound and its rhythm.

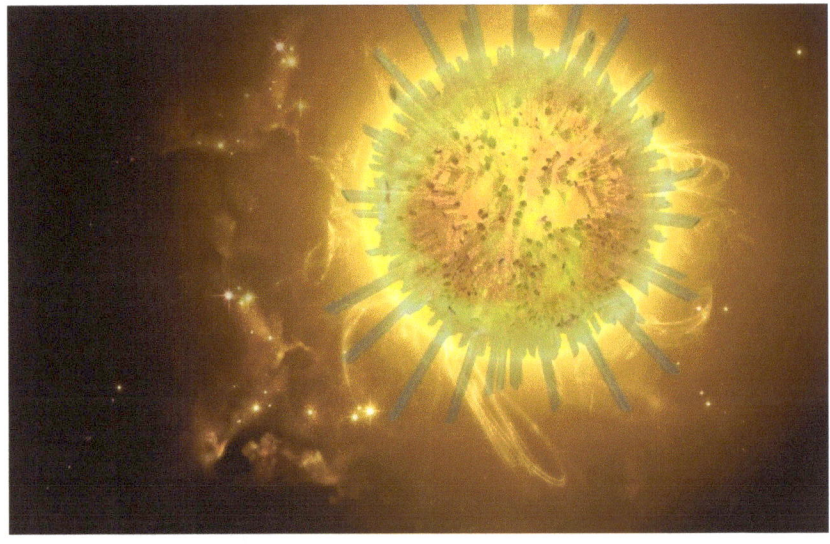

Ensuring that his efforts were not in vain, Kozma positioned a thick plate next to the planet to achieve a more accurate adjustable frequency, allowing his compositions to

The Creator of the Universe

be heard throughout the universe—given, of course, that his creation was placed in a high dimension.

The Cladnis organized themselves with great enthusiasm around the grand organ, ready to play their first musical composition consisting of multiple movements. Percussion, wind, and string instruments accompanied the symphony, positioning Musa as The Musical Center of the Universe, regulating the rhythm of the constellations.

The Gods fixed their eyes on the conductor, taken aback by how much beauty could come from such a tiny being.

"The shift in our spirits caused by this euphony is immeasurable." The Creator felt like a proud father.

Losna's inability to stand still signaled that it was now time for her creation. Like a mother-baby connection, she gently massaged her belly, gravitating the spheres towards her. Increasing in sizes in response to the maternal touch, the spheres intersected in her stomach, giving birth to Argyris.

The planet was made up of two identical parts intersecting one another. The inhabitants were surrounded by a variety of auras in all forms and colors, which was how they differentiated themselves.

Aware of the symmetry and the existence of their soul mate, they spent their lives searching for each other. Soul mates came together to help awaken one another and remind them of who they are. However, it was imperative that they first be ready, both spiritually and emotionally, before seeking out his or her soul mate; otherwise, it would lead to an unhappy relationship.

The recognition of the soul mate was often found in the eyes, as well as their voices. The soul mate's eyes seemed to pull them in, while the sound of their voices struck a familiar chord. Finally, when the blissful encounter took place, the soul mates were triggered with electromagnetic waves, linking them for all eternity. These events raised the temperature of the planet, creating rings of love so radiant that could be spotted in distant galaxies, placing Argyris as The Central Sun of Love.

"Bringing this kind of conscious love to light is a gift for all to see," the Creator boasted proudly over Losna's creation.

Brahman's breathing intensified. After having seen Losna's creation, he had no doubt that if they had been given the chance to live in Argyris, they would have been soulmates. He imagined the encounter with Losna, how his eyes connected as their bodies were about to touch when a sudden airflow knocked the hood of his cloak backwards, bringing him to reality.

Like in breeding season, the upward force of Celare's wings enveloped the two spheres. Sharing his body heat, he parted his outer feathers and pressed his warm bare tummy against the spheres. The incubation temperature increased, successfully bringing to life the new creation.

Planet Chromos had a crystalline solid surface with geometrical shapes, consisting of snowflakes, diamonds, and salt. The optical spectra of the crystals formed a multi-colored halo around Chromo, two times wider than the planet itself.

Many microscopic crystals fused together into a single solid mass, bringing the first inhabitants to life: The Orbs. These "light balls" appeared in a variety of different shapes, sizes, and colors, carrying celestial bodies in their evolution. These angelic beings could move from one place to another without passing through any in between places. This ability allowed them to appease the wishes and hopes of many in the universe. As a sign of a granted wish, nebulas were expelled into the universe, raising The Universal Hope.

The vast luminous nebulas seen at a distance baffled the Gods as the painter impressed his love of garish colors upon the universe. Kozma applauded with euphoria, jumping up and down whenever a nebula was spotted making a masterful entrance into the cosmos.

"With the presence of The Orbs, the inhabitants of all creations will be well protected, Bravo Celare..." The Creator was motionless until a curtain of water served as a welcome distraction.

"Well then, I suppose it's time for my creation!" Astra held the spheres high, intersecting them. Her hair began to expand with no end in sight, becoming waves in a wild ocean, inviting a great swirl to wrap the scene. A body of water produced by the meeting of opposing currents created a vortex with a downdraft ending in the new creation of Kallis.

The planet was completely covered by two oceans that meet, but never mix. The Ocean of Faith was turquoise and very dense because of its high concentration of salt, while the

The Creator of the Universe

Ocean of Souls was completely translucent and made of fresh water. Distinguishing the merge of the two great bodies of water were millions of golden eggs, forming a belt around the planet.

Two different species hatched from these eggs. The Kommos belonged to the Ocean of Faith; these beings could be described as elongated blue fish. Similar to a dolphin, they used high-pitched sound waves to communicate through different dimensions. On the other hand, the beings from the Ocean of Souls were the sensitive Kamusis. With the head and upper body of a human and the tail of a fish, these creatures lured all living things with their enchanting voices. At the center of their forehead, they had a birthmark called a Kukum, a circular crystal that transmitted emotion through song.

The Kommos and the Kamusis worked together, reflecting the power of consciousness through wisdom and harmony.

"Well, it all seems too... perfect." YinYang said, interrupting everyone's clear fascination with these creatures.

"Too perfect? What does that mean?" asked the Creator, concerned.

"If you would allow me to show you what I'm referring to," YinYang replied, deviously. His golden opportunity had arrived.

Stretching his muscular arms, YinYang slipped his cunning fingers upon the spheres. With his right hand, he squeezed one of the spheres, manipulating it with his fingertips. "Mmm... what if...." His eyes revealed a suspicious plan taking force, reinforced by the strangeness of Kozma's music.

Determined to win, YinYang knew he had to create something extraordinary if he wanted to catch the Creator's

The Creator of the Universe

attention. With one more squeeze, he changed the right sphere into a tetrahedron.

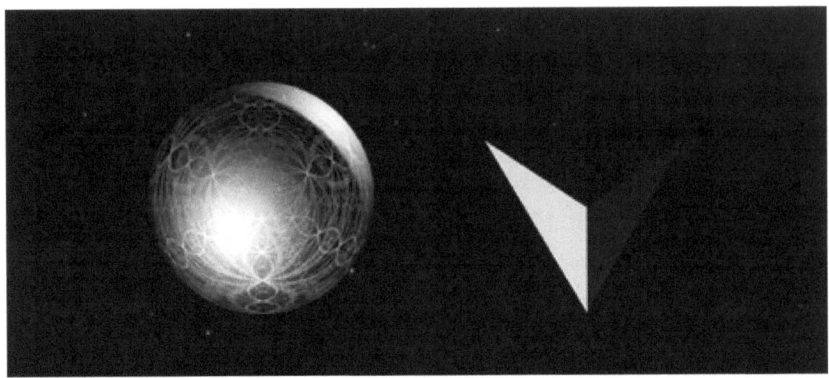

It was no surprise for the Creator that YinYang would do something different, but he was heavily deviating from the rest. For a moment, the Creator felt the need to stop him, but he could not interfere as that was the agreement.

Very sure of himself and making sure to avoid doing the same thing as his companions, he placed the tetrahedron upside down entirely inside the sphere so that the two shapes were combined, unlike the previous creations in which only the midpoints intersected.

No one was prepared for what happened next. The empty space between the sphere and the tetrahedron created a hologram, which created an illusion in the understanding of the whole and knowledge from the sphere.

Planet Tellus arose, contained within the tetrahedron. This caused a misunderstanding of reality since two spheres did not create it. Time in a sphere does not exist because the center of a sphere is equidistant from all edges. Nevertheless, when YinYang created the tetrahedron, its three sides shaped time as a succession of the past, present, and future. The tetrahedron itself prevented the beings living there from understanding time as an infinite present. YinYang had taken his creations' sight and forced them to live in a long dream, with a false interpretation of reality.

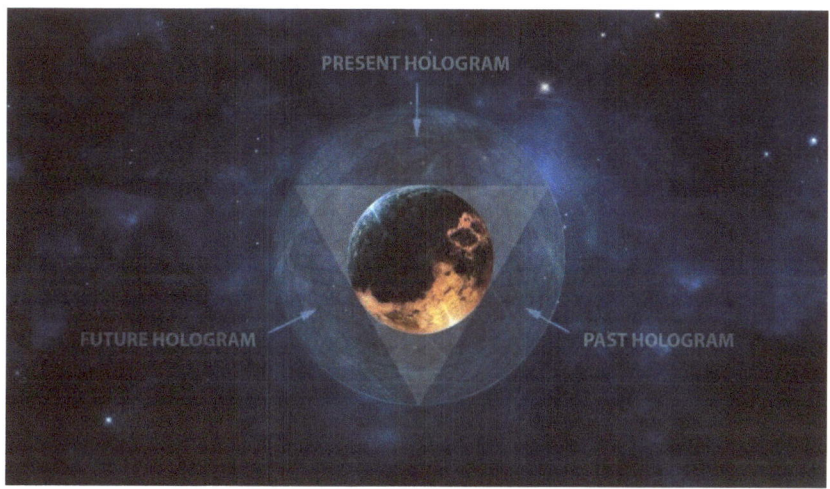

Absolutely everything that occurred on Tellus was in opposites, black and white, hot and cold, good and bad, with endless contrasts.

Only half of the planet received the sun's rays at any time. On Tellus' illuminated side, direct solar radiation struck, creating hot deserts with reddish rocks forming at high temperatures. On the opposite side of the planet, were eternal nights with cold winds, freezing the inhabitants' to their very core. In an attempt to survive these extremes, the inhabitants of Tellus positioned themselves along the junction of the two halves, trying to find a balance in temperature.

The inhabitants on Tellus were also created as two different beings. Those who originated from the sphere were feminine, thin and blessed with the gift of procreation. In contrast, those created from the tetrahedron were masculine, driven by strength and direction. Similar to the others' creations, the inhabitants of Tellus could breed, but not indefinitely, because of their perception of time. The tetrahedron's illusion forced them to live a lifespan of about ninety years. After this time, their soul would return to the sphere, allowing them to live in the infinite present before returning to Tellus to repeat this cycle.

"This is all for what?" the Creator asked, no longer bothering to hide his concern. "How are these beings supposed to evolve in such a short span of time? What makes you think that these beings would want to return to a place like Tellus, after being exposed to the infinite present of the sphere?"

He had no way of answering these questions. For the first time, he was worried and at a loss for words. *What if the inhabitants refused to stay in Tellus, wishing to live in the sphere instead? My planet would become desolate, and I would have failed.* His thoughts became jumbled. *It is likely that no being will wish to return to Tellus if they still have access to the knowledge they gained from the sphere. If I force them to stay in Tellus, they will simply do whatever is necessary to spend as little time as possible in this creation of mine, leaving it completely uninhabited.*

"Ah, I know," his eyes now opened like a hunter upon seeing his prey. "I will place a great magnet in the center of the planet, called the Great Magnet of Forgetfulness. This will attract the memories of the inhabitants at birth, leaving their memories frozen. All the information will be there, but it will be unattainable. This memory loss will be temporary, lasting only as long as their lives on Tellus, and they will regain full consciousness once they return to the sphere."

"YinYang, you have condemned these creatures to a life of false reality, without even giving them the chance to attain absolute consciousness!" The Creator struggled to catch his breath.

YinYang was aware that things had spiraled out of control, and he would have to justify his actions. "Not entirely, my Creator. These beings will put forth great effort

The Creator of the Universe

to surpass various lessons and experiences. When they have evolved enough, they will make a huge leap within their consciousness, generating a change in their perception, causing the pyramid to change shape. The next shape will be the cube of the fourth dimension, and so on, until finally they achieve the sphere with infinite dimensions."

"Don't you think it would have been wiser to give these people the infinite wisdom of the sphere from the start? This knowledge belongs to them," the Creator did not hide his disgust.

"I beg your pardon, my Creator, but don't you think there is more merit in coming into a world where you know nothing, forcing yourself to achieve true knowledge through your own efforts? My classmates provided their creations with perfection; I provided mine with free will. I believe there is more value in this, don't you think?" YinYang's question was not a question at all.

The Creator closed his eyes, hoping that when he opened them, he would wake from a horrible nightmare. He felt as if he had failed himself as well as YinYang.

With his head bowed down Kozma stared at the Creator while holding his hand. Kozma's eyes looked like two icicles thawing. His tears ran endlessly onto his cheeks, and his inverted smile could not hide the sadness. For a moment, he felt like composing a melody to make the Creator feel better, but he was sure that it would not come out exactly a happy one.

The silence grew unbearable, and the disciples looked at each other with deep concern. Only Brahman truly understood the Creator's pain, and he wished more than anything that he could trade places with him to take on this betrayal.

Slowly, the Creator steadied his breathing to control the heartache that now took a hold of him. "Explain something to me, YinYang. How will your creations know right from wrong, seeing that they lack absolute knowledge?"

"Very simple! They will learn by contrast, which is why I have created both good and bad. They are one in the same, but manifest themselves differently. For example, Tellus is half-cold and half-hot; both are temperatures but at different extremes. The same goes for love and hate; both are emotions but expressed differently. I could give you many more examples."

"More examples?" exclaimed the Creator. "The more I try to understand you, YinYang, the less I really do. How do you expect the Telluranians to evolve by contrast if every time they return with the ultimate knowledge of the sphere to live their next lives, they have it taken from them? This is not a journey to evolution; it is simply filling a vase with water and emptying it repeatedly yet expecting the flowers to grow. What's the point?"

YinYang tried to come up with a quick excuse but could not. "I have to admit to you, I didn't fully think out that little detail." YinYang avoided his Creator's gaze.

"That 'little detail,' as you call it, has doomed these beings to live an extremely hostile life. They are destined to believe that this world of polarity is all that exists. For the first time, I understand what sadness is, YinYang, and you have shown it to me." The Creator's face grew pale, and his eyes looked like crystals filled with tears

3

The Intervention of the Gods

More than embarrassed, YinYang felt like a failure, defeated by his own ego. He did not know what to say, so he watched the Creator out of the corner of his eye while the others looked for a solution to the problem he had created.

"If you would allow me, my Creator," Brahman interrupted. "You did say that we could offer help among ourselves. We may not be able to change what happened, but we can surely do something about this matter."

"The universe and I thank you for any help you are able to offer. I'm sure YinYang will be thankful as well." The Creator looked pointedly at him.

Nothing seemed to matter to YinYang, who placed himself with his light side facing his classmates so they would not notice his dark side smiling. He was sure that none of them understood the concept of polarity as well as he did.

Brahman, Losna, Astra, Kozma, and Celare placed themselves around Tellus, carefully studying every detail in the hopes of finding a clue to a solution. Kozma could not help but always be at the very front, never failing to humor his classmates. He once again positioned his ears as if ready to conduct and composed a beautiful harmony. As it entered the hologram of Tellus, he played,

The Creator of the Universe

> "Round and round like a drum,
> Light and dark spin around the sun,
> Taking turns in this great dance,
> To give birth to balance."

Kozma's vibrations forced Tellus to begin spinning on its own axis, allowing each half of the planet to spend equal amounts of time in sunlight and darkness, creating balanced temperatures. Then, something unexpected happened. Because the hologram was, in reality, just empty space, the vibrations of his sound expanded beyond than expected, generating a series of events. Not only did Tellus begin spinning on its own axis, but so did the eleven surrounding planets, each beginning to rotate around a central sun, like dancers.

"How odd," Kozma said, hoping that this effect had not jeopardized Tellus. He did not understand how the rules of space worked within a three-dimensional world. It was like learning to crawl after having to run.

"Do not worry, my son. You have done well. These beings will at least have a more suitable place to live." The Creator's face lit up a little in the midst of these unfortunate times.

Suddenly, they all heard a splash. Astra was cupping her hands above Tellus, holding a vast amount of water, which she slowly released to keep the inhabitants of Tellus safe. To her surprise, the water fell right through the planet. Astra stood motionless for a moment; her confidence disappeared. "What had just happened?"

Brahman interrupted her. "If you would allow me, I think I can be of some help, my beloved Astra." A sense of relief washed over her. She trusted him.

It was the first time that Brahman had intervened. He stared directly at Astra and asked her to join both hands over

The Creator of the Universe

Tellus as he transmitted his thoughts as verses into the hologram:

> "Over Tellus, water rains
> Changing geometry to sustain
> Salinity increasing in its composition
> Greater density as the solution."

Astra let the water fall in droplets. This time, the water landed on the planet's surface, adapting and forming beautiful oceans and rivers. Increasing the density of the water had enabled the hologram to sustain it.

As Astra stared at the oceans, she was hit with a feeling of nostalgia. She feared that her beautiful contribution would never be fully appreciated without its true inhabitants. So, she went to Kallis looking for help. "My dear Kommos and Kamusis, I apologize for my interruption, but I need to ask you a favor. Our fellow Telluranians have been affected by an unfortunate turn of events, and they need our help."

YinYang was lost in his own thoughts, but he could still hear his classmates trying to fix the mess he had created. He enjoyed watching them beg their own creations for help. *They will not be able to fix it. No one understands polarity the way I do,* he again thought, with a smirk.

Astra continued. "It is not an order. If you wish not to partake, I will understand."

Dauphin, the chief of the Kommos, and Siren, the leader of the Kamusis, offered their services immediately. "You can count on us, Astra. It's the least we can do after you created this beautiful home for us."

The Kommos were experts in inter-dimensional communication. Dauphin sent potent sound waves to Tellus, trying to gain a mental image of the planet, but when the waves reached Tellus they passed through without detecting any solid surface. He had never communicated with a planet in such a low dimension, which frustrated him. Finally, he realized that the only way to communicate with Tellus was to enter its three-dimensional reality, which would allow him to understand how sound waves worked in a lower dimension.

"Attempting to help them from here, dear Astra, would be like trying to help you cross an ocean of sand. We simply do not understand their concept of reality. I will travel to Tellus. It's the only way to help them," Dauphin said, as he looked over at Lumba, his partner.

"Then we will go together," Lumba was determined to stay together no matter what happened.

This noble gesture touched Astra's heart. The Kommos and the Kamusis were very united—so much so that Siren immediately offered to go as well.

The leaders were ready to leave, and only them. They would have never exposed their young generation to such a dangerous mission. It was a thought that would never even cross their mind. The wisest must set the example. With great knowledge, comes great responsibility.

Astra had mixed feelings about this. "I don't think this is a good idea. I would never put you in harm's way." She was very thankful for their kind gesture, but felt that allowing them to go to such a low dimension would not be safe for them.

Dauphin and Siren responded in harmony. "With all due respect, we take responsibility for our own actions. We are aware that this journey has risks, but we can be sure of one thing: We will show the Telluranians the knowledge that awaits them, allowing them to expand their very limited horizons."

Astra was filled with such pride that had she known how to cry, she would have inundated the entire universe with her tears. She held them by their hands as she spoke,

The Creator of the Universe

> "Your minds and hearts shall be
> Inundated with the waters of mystery
> The Kommos and Kamusis will reveal
> All the knowledge and emotions we feel."

Astra felt her heart break as she placed Kommos and Kamusis in the waters of Tellus—the way a mother does when she is parted from her children.

A comforting hand rested on her shoulder, "Thank you, daughter of mine. I know how hard that must have been," the Creator said with great pain.

This situation had deeply affected them all—except for YinYang, whose devious smiled made it seem like the universe was getting too small to hide his joy.

Looking at Tellus, Celare could not stand to see a place so bland and low-spirited. Absolutely everything was either black or white.

"What horror! This is a disgrace to art!"

Not only did Celare dislike what he saw, but it also saddened him that there were beings who had to live in such a miserable place. With his characteristic rainbow flight, he observed Tellus' surroundings very carefully and said:

> "Orbs fly across the sky
> Releasing arts of colors as they glide
> Bringing Tellus back to life
> With color and happiness there to guide."

Once Celare's contribution had settled upon Tellus, it was as if every color in a painter's palette had been thrown onto a white canvas. The ocean sparkled in every shade of blue. The leaves on the trees now had vibrancy to them, adjusting their colors to the seasons. Every flower resembled a frozen flame.

"This is stunning, Celare. You truly have a unique gift for beauty," the Creator said in amazement.

Despite their impressive contributions, the gods now faced an even greater challenge: helping the Telluranians themselves. Their hopes now lay with Losna and Brahman.

"Brahman, you haven't been given the chance to make your own creation. I think it's time, don't you?" Losna asked with a persuasive smile.

Brahman choked nervously on his words and he could only manage an "Aaaakk." Having her so close prevented him from producing a coherent answer.

The Creator had to turn this time to hide his laughter, *looking at this son of mine in love I have to admit is very funny. He behaves more childish than Kozma.*

Slyly, Brahman clear his throat while trying to regain control of his feelings, as well as his thoughts. He was carefully planning his creation, but his thoughts kept returning to Tellus. He realized that his mind did not hold the space for a new creation and he felt selfish knowing that the Telluranians were destined to fail. He continued to wander. *If I use the two spheres, I will create a reality with absolute knowledge, preventing me from entering Tellus' reality. However, if I do as YinYang did, I will create the same problem, leading us right back to where we started.*

Brahman took in a heavy breath, but this time he thought aloud, "If I repeat what YinYang did, but with the vertex of the tetrahedron facing upward, this would give the Telluranians a spiritual body or a spiritual reality. Unlike the tetrahedron that YinYang placed pointing down, which only gives them a physical body or a physical reality."

His face suddenly lit up, "My Creator, the inversion of the new tetrahedron could serve as a connection between the people of Tellus and the reality of the sphere. Seeing that

The Creator of the Universe

Tellus is founded based on polarity, this should work given that it is the opposite. Even though I cannot anticipate the result, I do believe this to be the best possible solution. I ask for your permission to continue, my Creator."

"I have trusted you since the day I laid eyes on you, my son." The Creator instilled such trust in him that he knew whatever decision he made would be the best for Tellus.

They all heard a slight grunt from YinYang. He was making it very clear that he was growing uncomfortable, making Brahman even more certain of his decision.

Brahman felt the weight of the universe fall on his shoulders, but this would not stop him. With trembling hands he held the spheres. Carefully, he repeated YinYang's exact steps except for the tetrahedron, which he turned pointing up. With a deep breath, he slowly intersected them and placed the new creation within the center of Tellus.

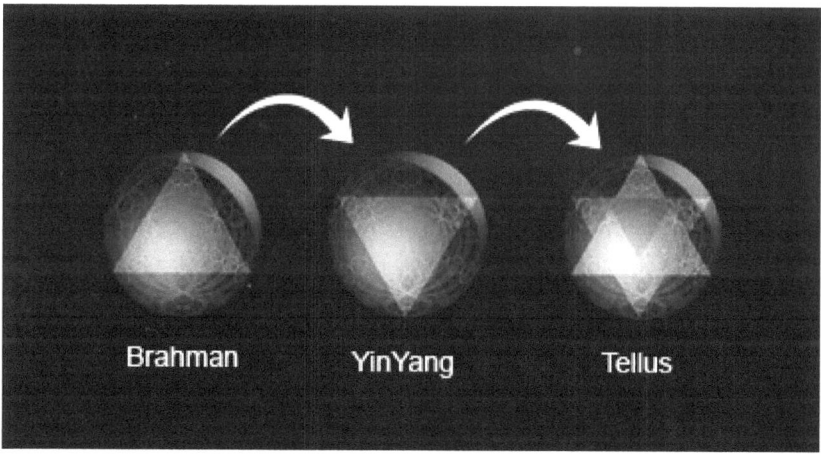

The temperature around Brahman's creation increased, producing a geometric energy as the two pyramids intersected. They spun with great speed in opposite directions, giving rise to the star tetrahedron.

The Creator of the Universe

Brahman's plan appeared to be working; from that moment on, the Telluranians had free access to connect themselves to the reality of the sphere. However, they continued to behave the same as before without seeking the absolute knowledge they could now access. They were as lost as ducklings with no mother to follow.

The disciples were dumbfounded and full of questions. "I simply don't understand how this happened. I have provided them with the ultimate knowledge. Why don't they just use it?" Brahman tried to hide his disappointment, but failed.

"My dear friend," said Losna, "You have done an excellent job, but Tellus is a very odd place. From what I see, the energy of polarity is so strong that it has blinded them. Any information they have not acquired on their own is foreign to them. I think I can help, if you allow me."

Brahman was in shock. Losna had never spoken this much to anyone, and even more had never shown this much kindness. His eyes gave away his confusion, but he was hopeful nonetheless. "Of course... thank you, Losna," he said with a trembling voice.

Losna returned to her confident, yet mysterious manner, placing herself before Tellus. Rubbing her belly, her brows furrowed in concentration. Her eyes darted to each detail of the scene. Out her belly flew a miniature moon, hanging like a great luminous pearl on the radiant breast of the universe. Carefully she placed it close to Tellus:

> "Through dreams the moon will shine
> To show Telluranians the lie in their minds
> Drop by drop the truth will glow
> To show the way as they go."

Losna had created the moon, which hypnotized the Telluranians with its strength and magnetism, making it impossible for them to resist the sleep that Losna had given them. The Telluranians began to sleep an average of eight hours a day, during which they established a connection with their higher self at a very profound level. This connection became so deep that their memory was only capable of retaining an insignificant amount of this information once they woke up.

The eyes of the universe were on Tellus. Losna's solution was providing results, as some Telluranians were obtaining the information of the spirit. However, once these beings awoke, they simply doubted the information given. It was as if they thought it was an illusion, when ironically, the illusion was their reality. The Telluranians only believed what they could physically see, and any information not perceived by their human eyes was simply disregarded.

Losna's magnetism diminished. "Don't be sad, my dear Losna," said Brahman. "Your creation provided results, and now there is only one thing left to do."

Losna lifted her eyes to meet his, despairing. "One thing? If the Telluranians chose not to believe, what is left to do?"

Brahman tightened his jaw, as if what he was about to do took every last bit of his strength. With a deep breathe, he faced his classmates, addressing the Creator. "I gave my creation to Tellus, and I now have the responsibility to find a solution in the same way my classmates have done, correct?"

"Yes," responded the Creator, confused by Brahman's question.

"Very well. My solution may require much risk, but I give you my word that it will cause the majority of Telluranians to believe in the truth of spirit," Brahman said with an unreadable expression.

The Creator was suspicious, and Brahman's stare made him uneasy. "Stop, Brahman! I do not know what you have in mind, but it's unnecessary to put yourself at risk. I will accept solutions, but under no circumstance will any children of mine put themselves in danger!"

"You said you've believed in me since the day you laid eyes on me. Now is no different," Brahman said with such assurance that the Creator knew there was no persuading him. His mind was set,

> "The star tetrahedron I will create
> Merkaba it shall be named
> I will travel to Tellus' reality
> To show them wisdom and spirituality."

A beautiful figure appeared in front of him, it had a high vibration generated by the friction of the two opposite rotations of the tetrahedrons. He stepped inside the Merkaba and fixed his gaze upon Losna. At that moment, their glances merged into one and the only thing missing was the proximity of their bodies to seal their hearts.

The Creator of the Universe

"All I ask is that you come back safe," Losna's eyes swam with tears.

The Creator's face was washed blank with confusion, with his multiple turning eyes begging him to stop. He ran toward Brahman, but the force with which the Merkaba spun was too great. He only managed to exchange glances with Brahman before he disappeared from his sight.

The Gods saw a shock registered on the Creator's face. There was a silence in his soul and his brain stood still without projecting any light-images. Part of him was in pain. He felt a never-ending dark void that consumed everything. The Creator felt he would never be the same again.

4

Brahman Journeys to Tellus

With a knot in his stomach, Brahman directed the Merkaba to the center of Tellus. Around him it became so bright that it could rival the sun itself. Everything felt different. He was discovering bodily sensations for the first time as he floated in a warm, and surprisingly comforting, liquid.

Where am I? Why do I perceive temperature within my body? What are those noises?

Slowly, the space in which he found himself grew smaller, and he began to feel uncomfortable. "I'm trapped. I wish to leave!" He tried to yell. In response, a force of gravity pulled at him, the same way Losna did. Could it be possible? Could this be coming from her?

He felt both a pressure and the sensation of being pulled by his head. "Help!"

Suddenly his body was revealed to the unknown. The liquid that had provided him with a sense of heat was gone, replaced by a cold blanket covering him.

Why do I feel so sick? Needing to be heard, Brahman tried to communicate, but all that came out was a loud cry. He moved his eyes in all directions, searching for an answer. Noises engulfed him, accompanied with many unknown faces that appeared and disappeared, but only one hypnotized him. A sweet face approached him with a look that hugged him to the soul, the way a mother's lullaby does. Her proximity was the only thing that gave him comfort. *What a strange feeling. I do not know her and I love her already. Even more so, I feel like I need her.*

He tried to communicate with his thoughts, but he received no response, just noises in reply. *Why doesn't she understand me? What do these strange noises mean?*

He quickly learned that when he cried, he gained something in return: a beautiful smile, a warm hug, food, comfort, a melody. *Hmm. I guess I will have to stick to this pattern until I manage to communicate with these people around me, especially with the one I love the most.*

The days passed, and Brahman noticed that certain words were repeated at a high frequency. He decided to try to imitate these sounds, and after several attempts, he finally managed to form similar sounds. In return, he received applause. There was one word in particular that when spoken, caused the person who made him feel the happiest come near him. "Mom."

Brahman had much to do, but it was not until he realized that every single thing, person, and place had a specific name that he understood the complexity of his mission and the amount of time it would take. Quite often Brahman's parents saw him breathe in deeply, as if there was something he wanted to say, not realizing that their son was no ordinary boy.

With time, they learned that his behavior and knowledge did not correlate to those of a child his age. They thought he was intelligent beyond reason, but as the years passed, his gifts turned into something much more.

Brahman answered to a different name on Tellus: Mester. For both his mother, Hazar, and father, Domino, it was nearly impossible to keep a low profile with Mester as a son. He could not help but call attention to himself between his curiosity and the types of comments he made. By the age of eight, he was tutoring others in arithmetic, algebra, and geometry at a doctorate level. Mester's information was much too advanced for his time, causing people to doubt the validity of his knowledge. As word spread about this peculiar little boy, huge masses of people, including important figures, sought him out in hopes of learning from him.

Mester lived in Tallen, in a humble home. The entrance door was spotted with years of water damage and its creaking noise made sure no doorbell was needed. Inside it was a living museum, highlighting a golden wall clock from Hazar's mother, reminding them of her presence with every chime. The walls were made of mud, bearing the bony impressions of fingers belonging to those who built it.

"Remember, my love, when we built this home?" Hazar asked.

"Yes, I do, but more, I remember the love with which we made it," Domino would respond, nostalgically.

Mester could not have asked to grow up in a more loving home. That was one debt he owed destiny. The great pain he had felt being separated from his Creator was alleviated by the affection of his parents.

The house was upon the highest hill of Tallen, overlooking the town. From there, they could see what a maze the borough was, every house joined to the next. Of course, except for King Aldon's palace, with gold domed towers sufficiently exotic to inspire awe in the populous. At the back of the house was a porch with a long corridor, defined by a set of round columns linked to the next with a perfect archway. The stone floor appeared to have been laid down before any conception of a grid pattern. Almost camouflaged against the green and brown walls, were three old chairs, deformed by their many years of use. Gathering in them as a family every night after dinner was their definition of dessert. The refreshing breeze of the night carried the laughter and stories that they shared with much love and happiness.

Time seems to pass so slowly on Tellus, Mester thought as he blew out his eighteenth birthday candles.

The Creator of the Universe

Mester enjoyed the company of his friends, especially Lucia. She was a very special girl. Her black hair flowed down her back and shown like the sea at night. Her green eyes held such serenity making it impossible for anyone to not be held prisoner by them. Despite her inability to walk, she had an everlasting smile stained upon her lips. It was as if she was unaware of her current state. Her nobility and kindness was something that captivated Mester.

Mester's friends adored him for the unconditional care he always bestowed upon them. There was not a single classmate for whom he had not done a favor. As night fell, one by one, his friends returned home.

The sky was low and dark, filled with diamonds. With their energy drained, Domino and Hazar could not resist sitting outside to enjoy the warm summer breeze before going to sleep.

Whomp! Mester slammed the back door. "Mother, father, I wanted to thank you for my party, you always make feel at home."

"At home? This is your home my Son." Hazar replied bewildered.

"Do you know why I am here?" Mester asked with eyes about to reveal something.

Hazar always grew uneasy at the number of questions her son asked, and as the years passed, it grew more difficult for her to answer them.

"Hmm. I suppose to bring us much happiness," replied Domino, seeing that Hazar was at a loss for words.

"Yes, Father, but there is something more."

"It's getting late," his mother interrupted. "And you, sir, have to be up early for school."

"But, Mom, I already know everything they're going to teach me," Mester responded quickly.

"Say goodnight to your father, and go to sleep."

Domino hugged Mester, staring at Hazar trying to decipher the reason behind her reaction. He knew how perceptive she was, which reinforced that something was going on.

The next day, Domino still had those words Mester mentioned roaming in his thoughts. Seeing that Hazar was busy tidying up the house, Domino decided to accompany Mester to the banks of a nearby river, located just around the corner.

The river was so clear you could see the smoothness of the rocks underneath. Even though it was cold, they could not resist getting in, moving with robotic steps.

"Son, I wanted to continue our conversation from yesterday. Why are you here on Tellus?" he asked quietly, not completely sure he was ready for the response.

"Father, I think you have realized that I didn't come here to learn. I came here to teach the Telluranians of another truth, or better said another reality."

"What truth do you speak of, Mester?"

He was silent for a moment, picking his next words very carefully. *How do I explain this to my father without him having the necessary knowledge of geometry to understand the different levels of consciousness? How do I explain to him that time does not exist? This will be no easy task.* He shook his head from side to side.

"Father, do you think all that you see here is all that exists? That people pass away and that is the end of it? Do you really believe that the only purpose on this planet is to be born, grow old, and die? Don't you think there's a greater purpose to life?"

"Son, I asked you one question, and you respond with four more," Domino said with a weak smile, trying to hide his worry.

The Creator of the Universe

"My Father—the one who is up there in the universe, the Creator of everything you see, but who cannot be seen himself—is very worried about the people of Tellus."

"What do you mean by this, my son? I am your father."

"No, Father, I am referring to the father of us all, the Creator, to whom we owe this life to. He wants us to love each other unconditionally. But more importantly, he wants us to know the truth."

"What truth?" Domino asked, lightheaded.

"Tellus is destined for both good and evil, but if you choose the good, you will be able to transcend to a better world called... heaven." He decided to use this word instead of talking about the different dimensions and the reality of the sphere because his father did not look like he could take much more of the truth. "In heaven, you will enjoy eternal life."

"Eternal life? What is this heaven like? How do you know all this, Mester?"

"Father, if I told you how I came to be here, you would not understand. I would have to show you hundreds of equations and concepts of geometry, and even then, we would probably be right back to where we started. What I can tell you is that all Telluranians have access to the truth, but you are limited by your capacity to see it. If only you would all trust in what you feel."

"But, son, the truth you speak of, if we can't see it, how are we supposed to access it?"

"You have to believe. You have to have faith, and only then, will you be able to live a life worthy of living."

"What will happen to those who don't believe?" Domino asked, feeling overwhelmed.

"It will take them longer to attain the truth. It will become a repetitive cycle, like osmosis with no end. It would be like running a horserace around a track over and over, yet expecting the results to change."

"If the truth is the way you say it is, what rules must we follow for this change to take place?"

Mester was growing anxious. It was not that his father's questions were complicated, but rather that explaining these concepts in simple terms was no easy task.

"Father, here on Tellus, men dedicate themselves to the 'to do' rather than the 'to be.' Have you ever had an unexplainable feeling or sense about something only to notice after the fact that a certain event occurred, reassuring what you previously perceived? Alternatively, have you thought about someone and then run into them? The more you think about it, the more you write it off as a coincidence, right?"

"Right," Domino said almost immediately.

"Well, these feelings or senses are your subconscious knowledge guiding you, letting you know what road to take. Because there is no way for you to validate this knowledge, you doubt it, steering yourself away from its guidance. You also receive this intuition while you sleep, but you believe you are dreaming and that your dreams are insignificant."

"Why do we receive information in those manners, instead of in a more direct way?"

"Because this world you live in is not real. Everything is an illusion based on the very limited understanding of Telluranians themselves. The truth lies in the place I mentioned earlier called heaven, and you may only access this information with love, intuition, and faith."

"So, if the truth lies there, what are we doing here?"

Mester paused for a moment. He could see YinYang's devious smile rushing into his mind, but ultimately, he decided not to speak of his mistake. "I know it may not be ideal, Father, but you're here to make a great effort to attain this truth, from the darkness in which you find yourself.

The Creator of the Universe

Once you understand this, you will understand what comes next. In the first step, you must pretend that you're walking with a blindfold on, being guided only by your intuition, since your eyes will deceive you."

"Mester, have you spoken about this to anyone?" Domino asked, concerned.

"No, Father, but the time for that will come soon. This is my reason for being here."

A few seconds passed as Domino attempted to collect himself and his thoughts. He did not shift his gaze from his son. "Le–let's go home, son. It's getting late, and your mother must be worried."

Night came, but sleep did not come for Domino. He tossed and turned, thinking about what might happen when Mester decided to speak. He was scared of people's reactions, being aware that change does not come easily for others.

"Are you okay, my love? You seem restless," Hazar asked in her usual comforting way.

Domino knew that if he told her what Mester had said, neither of them would sleep that night. "Just going over things for tomorrow, love. That's all."

Mester awoke to the rooster's morning song. Still half asleep, Mester picked up his books, grabbed his morning cup of hot milk, and wrapped himself in his favorite sweater, knitted by his mother. The looping sound of the antique wall clock marked eight o'clock, time to leave for school. He asked his parents for their daily blessing and slung his backpack over just one shoulder as he ran to the door.

This particular morning, he felt different. The sky was consumed with numerous shades of gray and black clouds, only giving a break for a narrow ray of light targeting Pastor Joel's temple. Mester was heading down his usual route to school but his mind was not following the road. Something within him pushed him in the direction of the temple. *Well...*

I guess it would not be the end of the world if I arrive late to school just one time.

When he approached the temple, he noticed an unusual conglomeration of people. *It could be that Pastor Joel is giving a sermon, but why outside the temple?*

An intense cry of pain pinched his skin. It was so strong that he felt it deep within his soul. After taking in the sea of sad faces around him, he knew that something serious had just occurred. Using his shoulders as a shield, he made his way to the front of the crowd.

Sophia, Lucia's mother, was crying inconsolably over her daughter's body. Her scream was ferocious, "Mester she is gone. She has left us!"

The impression of the lifeless body blinded Mester for a moment, her young age failed to announce any kind of farewell. His eyes locked upon Lucia's inert body, her skin went pale, and even her lips were barely there. Mester was exceptional with everyone, but with Lucia, it was something much more. It could have been said that Losna had competition in Tellus.

Lucia was lying on the damp ground, next to the fountain. Mester fell to his knees, picking up her hand, so cold and pale. His pain was too great, the muscles of his chin trembled like a small child as he look up to the sky in search of the Creator as well as his companions. *If you can hear me, I ask you to help her. I understand that it is a normal process in Tellus, but please give her the opportunity to live a long life filled with happiness as a reward for her nobility.*

At that moment, the air pushed against his face, it felt like the heavens were knocking at his door. Within seconds, big pellets of water from the fountain spat at the crowd.

This feeling of being wet.... It was all too familiar to Mester. He had no doubt that Astra was behind this.

Shuddering through the cold that his damp clothes had brought upon him, Mester took Lucia by both hands in hopes of pulling her up. "Come on Lucia, open your eyes and look at how beautiful of a day it is." The sun shined so brightly that it managed to dissipate every cloud within the sky.

Sophia looked at Mester with a confused look upon her face. She thought Mester had lost his mind.

Suddenly, the inert body came to life, stretching as if in bed and had just awakened from a long sleep.

Lucia sat up and held Sophia and Mester by the arm. "Help me get up now. I do not want to be lying down anymore." She got up, but her mother was worried about having the wheelchair ready for her to sit in.

"Mother, I don't need the chair anymore." Sophia remained motionless until she saw Lucia walk up next to Mester.

"It's a miracle!" People shouted.

Sophia fell to her knees with tears of joy running down her cheeks. She was waving her hands to the sky thanking the heavens.

"Mester, thank you for what you have done. I will never be able to repay you," Sophia cried with endless tears.

Mester was at a loss for words since, in reality, he had nothing to do with this "miracle". It had all been Astra's doing.

That moment of joy became a sign of salvation for many witnesses suffering from illness. The crowd flowed down toward Mester, while he opened his arms as a shield to protect Lucia.

"Help me, Mester, I have had a pain in my back ever since I can remember. Heal me, please!"

"Please save my mother, for she is dying!"

Mester was breathing in and out but air wouldn't enter his lungs. At last, he saw a familiar face that allowed him to take in his first deep breath.

"Son, what are you doing here? You should be in school!" Domino fought his way through the crowd. "What happened?" Seeing how frantic the crowd was, he took Mester by the arm and rushed him home.

When Hazar saw Domino walk into the house, pale and pulling Mester by the arm, her intuition screamed at her. "Dear, there is something you must know. Go on, Mester. Tell your mother."

Hazar was not interested in listening, or maybe she was once again evading her intuition. She immediately rushed to the kitchen to make two cups of hot tea. Mester followed her and pulled her into a hug. Locking eyes with her, he said, "Mother, I am sorry for not attending school today, but Lucia was about to die. I only wanted to help. Is that wrong of me?"

"No, my son. Helping others is not wrong." Her eyes were watering.

"Then, why do you cry, Mother?"

"I cry because I fear for you. I don't want you to be in any danger."

"Mother, in this world, it is inevitable for good and bad things to happen. That is part of the chaos behind the creation of Tellus. However, in that chaos, we find signs to lead us out. That is why I have come, to help you see these signs."

Domino interrupted. "What signs are you talking about, son?"

"This morning on my way to school, the sky was odd, and its color was unusual. The air had a different smell to it, and that is when I saw a ray of light making its way through the clouds illuminating the temple of Pastor Joel, as if it were trying to tell me something. If I had ignored this sign from my intuition and listened to the logic telling me to go to school, Lucia would not be among us now. Don't get me wrong, I'm not saying that going to heaven is bad, but it would be wrong to leave without having learned your lesson, ultimately forcing you to return repeating the cycle again."

"Lesson? Heaven? Racing? I can't listen to any of this!" Hazar looked for comfort by covering her ears, trying to silence her surroundings.

"I think it has been a long day. Let's all take a walk down to the river and forget about our worries. What do you think?" Domino asked in hopes of easing the tension in the room, but his attempts were put on hold as a banging on the door broke the silence in the room. Domino ran to the window to find not one person at the door, but hundreds of people seeking Mester.

"Don't leave. Stay here. Everything will be fine." Domino exited through the back door to make sure that no one would enter.

Once outside, he addressed the crowd. "What do you want? Why the ruckus?" The people immediately voiced their concerns and wishes.

"My mother is sick, and I need your son to cure her!"

"My son cannot walk, he needs a miracle!"

"My mother was evicted. Please help her!"

Domino was heartbroken as he stared into the hurt eyes of each person. He tried to pick the right words to say, but before he opened his mouth, another voice answered.

"I know the great hurt you're all enduring, and I will help you all with the healing process," Mester said. "I will teach every one of you how to be your own healers. You all have the power to heal yourselves. Those of you who wish to learn, I will gladly teach you. Come to Calypso River tomorrow when the rooster calls, and I will give you all my first lesson."

In the silence, there was general agreement, and the crowd dissipated. Nevertheless, the great fear that Domino and Hazar had suppressed for so long now began to grow.

Night came, and the insomnia now fell on both parents. Every muscle in their faces were tense and in-between tosses, their eyes would meet without a word, communicating the intense fear alive in their hearts.

The rooster finally cried, but the sound was different this morning and not as enjoyable as it had once been. They could hear Mester's hurried footsteps in the kitchen.

"Son, I don't think you should go." Domino begged.

"Father, if I asked you for help, would you deny me?"

"Of course not!"

"Well, they are the children of my Father, the Creator of all. They are our brothers and sisters, and we cannot abandon them in their times of need. Remember that love is based on appreciation, not possession." Every one of his words was so wise that it was impossible to argue.

"Despite our great fear for you, we will support you, my son." Domino cleared his throat.

The slam of the door was the beginning of the tempest inside Domino and Hazar, hoping to somehow stop the storm to come.

5

Mester's Lessons

From the moment the light of the new day came, Mester knew it would be a great day. The birds were silhouettes against the beaming sun and the butterflies looked like flowers on the air.

As he neared the river, youthful spirits ran toward Mester to greet him, he had a great weakness for children.

"Good morning, my brothers and sisters. Thank you for coming. Today, I will give you a few guidelines to help you in your evolutionary process. I will number them, making it easier for you to recall the process."

He paused to observe the crowd, who waited, hanging on his every word. "Number one. Believe that there is someone mightier than you are. When we accept that there is a superior force, our Creator, we accept that we are a part of everything. Consequently, the knowledge that belongs to us will become more accessible."

The crowd erupted into questions. "What is the Creator like? What does he look like? Where does he come from? Why does he go by this name?"

"Slow down, my brothers and sisters. The questions you ask are insignificant details and only serve as distractions, allowing your eyes to betray and distract you from what is truly valuable. Physical descriptions are not what is important. What is important is to truly believe that the Creator exists in every one of you. We are a part of everything, and the healing energy originates from this idea."

Everyone was silent. Some stared at him with doubt, some with confusion, and others with enthusiasm to continue listening. "For now, I only ask you to listen and let this information sink in—not by reason but by the wisdom of your hearts,"

Mester continued his lecture. "Number two. Believe in your intuition. You must recognize that your intuition is the voice of your soul guiding you to make the right decision."

Immediately, the questions started. "What is intuition, Mester?"

"Intuition is the wisdom you can attain. It's the connection with your true selves and the ability to understand things immediately without the use of conscious reasoning."

A somewhat chubby, short man with a striking mustache could not contain his curiosity. "How do you use your intuition?" His name was Bruce; he was an arrogant man in charge of administering King Aldon's finances.

"Your intuition is that sudden feeling you get, regardless of what your head tells you, when you're faced with a decision. It's having certainty without logic."

"What about those of us who don't get that feeling?" Bruce adjusted his large black hat that he used to hide the fact that he was going bald.

"We all have intuition. To access it, we must learn to silence our minds—or at least learn to control them for our intuition to flourish."

Bruce lowered his eyebrows in efforts of masking his confusion. *How can I learn to silence my mind when I work for someone like the king?* He thought.

"Number three: Do not confuse knowledge with wisdom. Knowledge will help you survive on this planet, earn your bread, but wisdom will help you enjoy life after this one."

"Please give us an example, Mester," begged an elderly man.

"What is your name?"

"Simon, Sir"

"As you wish Simon. I will take two of you as an example." He motioned for Bruce and Simon to come forward. "I will ask each one of you two questions. Tell me, Bruce, how much do you make in a month?"

Domino and Hazar almost fainted from embarrassment. "Son, you can't ask those things!" Hazar pleaded with the boy.

"Then I won't be able to answer what they asked, Mother."

"It's okay, it's okay," Bruce said. "I have no problem answering this question. I make a lot of money, boy—around what ten of you here make a month." His voice was full of confidence.

"Are you happy?"

"Well, even though I lose sleep often and am quite stressed, I have everything I want."

Mester turned to ask Simon the same question, and the man giggled. "I don't know how much Bruce here thinks I make because I make nothing. I get by with the help of others, and I do favors in return. Now, if you are to ask me if I am happy, I most certainly am. I live life without worrying how to pay my house, food, and services. I don't know when or how I'll eat, or if I'll even make it yet another day, but somehow I always figure it out without ever losing sleep."

"Here's the response you're all looking for."

"We don't understand!" cried the audience.

"Here, you see a man who is happy because he has everything due to his knowledge. Simon is also happy even though he has nothing, but this is not true. He has the wisdom to know that one way or another, he will obtain what he needs for survival. Now, let me ask you, which man is happier? The one who needs more to be happy or the one who has little, but is also happy? Who is at greater risk of losing his happiness if he loses the material things in life?"

"Bruce!" yelled the crowd in unison.

"Good. See, those happiest are those who do not need much to be pleased, because they are the ones in charge of their own happiness."

"Number four: It's not enough to simply wish for things. You must also act on your wishes. On this point, I would like to give credit to Bruce."

Mester turned to the administrator, who seemed uncomfortable from the previous example. "If Bruce had only wished to become King Aldon's assistant and failed to study in order to achieve that, he wouldn't be where he is today."

Bruce's confidence seemed to race back to him.

"But, if Bruce got to where he is and now requires so many materialistic things to be happy, what's the point?" Domino wondered, not realizing he was actually speaking aloud. "Sorry, son, it was just a question I had."

"It's okay, Father, that's what I'm here for," Mester responded with a soothing smile. "I will summarize my three previous points. It is not bad to achieve your goals in life or to study or to push yourselves. What is bad are those goals that sacrifice your sleep and take over your happiness, those that dictate your life in a manner that makes you feel as if you have lost control over it. Bad is you ending up feeling enslaved on a race with no operator, a race that does not know how or when to stop. If you want to be happy while simultaneously achieving your goal, you must keep moving,

The Creator of the Universe

while being very attentive to the signals that this superior force sends to us along the way, letting us know when to accelerate or slow down through our intuition. Only then, are we guaranteed a successful and happy race, with the possibility of receiving a ticket of entry to a better world."

"What world is that?" asked the crowd.

"A world filled with truth, without the physical sufferings of Tellus. In the other world, your intuition will not be necessary because the truth will at last be open to you. Everything you'll see there will be the truth, and your eyes will no longer betray you, but will be loyal to your hearts," Mester explained the fourth dimension as best he could.

"You mean to say that the planet of Tellus is not real? How can that be? We can see it with our own eyes!"

"There is the greatest lesson you all must learn. Everything you see is a product of your imagination to such a point that it materializes itself. If you wish to cure yourselves from disease, which is what has brought you all here today, you will have to envision your own cure until it becomes a reality because you are the only ones in charge of the story that is your life."

"Then how did you help that little girl if she was supposed to cure herself?" David asked. He was a carpenter and a cousin of Domino.

"If you all learn to become the captain of a ship, does this mean you can't help a co-pilot who needs help? If the captain has the wisdom to teach, he or she should not just offer to help; it becomes an obligation to help those in need. Wisdom must always be used to help humanity as a whole prevail."

"What did you visualize when you helped that little girl?"

"Lucia's case was different. She came back from death and that has a different explanation. Let's just concentrate on how to heal yourselves for now," Mester said, deciding that giving them details about Astra and the other Gods would have only confused them further.

"You Telluranians have an aura formed by two tetrahedron, with one being inverted, called the Merkaba. The tetrahedron pointing up has a connection with the superior force of *to be* and the inverted pyramid pointing downward has a connection with an inferior force, which correlates with the one of Tellus, *to do*. For your body to be in balance, your superior and inferior energies must be working at the same intensity. Do you follow me now?"

"Yes!" responded the crowd with great excitement.

"Each tetrahedron has three zones that act like the control panel of a machine, signaling its level of performance in each one of these zones. When one or more of these zones is hindered, the velocity of the energy that radiates from it is affected. Consequently, the Merkaba stops functioning properly. We can make it work a little more, but its performance will not be the same, and the energy you will have to exert to keep it running will be far greater than what

The Creator of the Universe

is actually necessary. For example, have you ever asked yourselves why certain people manifest their wishes so easily? Well, the reason is that their Merkaba have their zones in balance, performing in the optimal condition."

"We have so many questions, Mester," murmured the crowd among themselves.

Simon could not hide his bewilderment, "How can we know what these zones are and how to repair them?"

"Just by looking at someone, I can identify these zones, but I will give you a few tips so you can practice. The three corners of the tetrahedron pointing down belong to the energy of *to do* and are made up of the brain, body, and action. Meanwhile, the tetrahedron that points upward is formed from the *to be* energy and is made up of love, intuition, and faith."

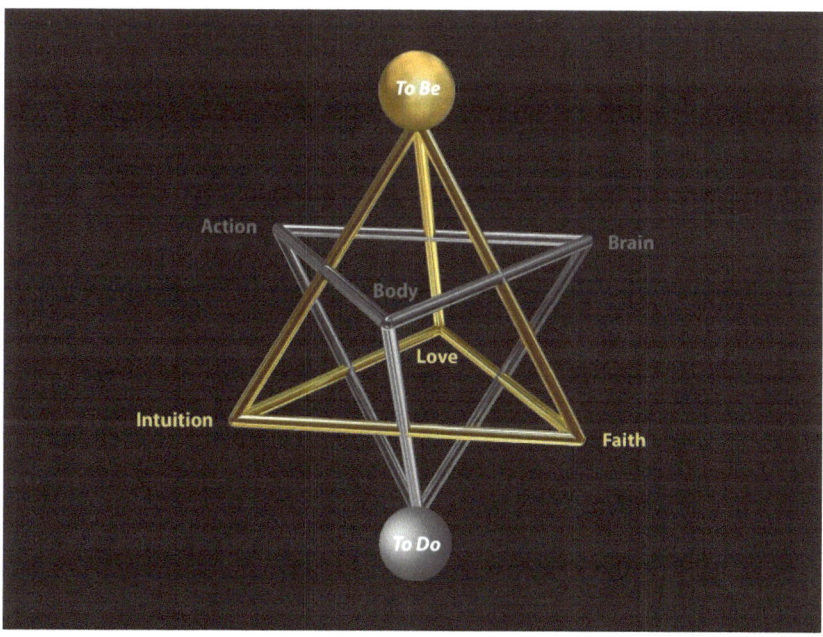

"To clarify this process, it is similar to that of a child going to school. At first, it will be difficult, but over time, it will become second nature. For now, you will not be able to see these zones, but you will be able to notice the consequences of your imbalance. For example, if a man talks very frequently directly from his brain, separated from his emotions, and only talks about his knowledge and not from wisdom, which zone do you think is putting his pyramid off balance?"

Bruce did not intend to answer this question as he was beginning to think this was personal.

Simon responded quickly. "The brain would be affected, and I imagine that the energy of *to do* would find itself in some trouble." The audience laughed.

"But then, what's the point in knowing this? How do we fix it?" Bruce asked, as if asking for his own personal solution.

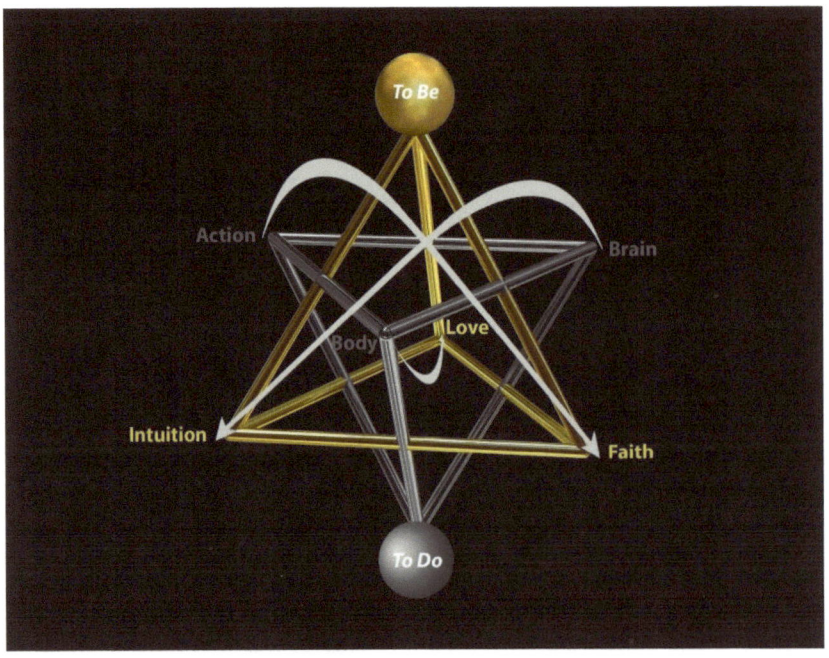

"It's very simple. When you envision the two tetrahedrons overlapping, you will see that the image now has six corners or zones. Since the zone of the brain is directly opposite from the zone of intuition, you simply have to learn to lower the velocity of your thoughts so the voice of your intuition can be heard with greater force, allowing for a balance between your brain and intuition."

Mester paused a moment to let his words sink in.

"Now, I will give you another example," he continued. "If a person isn't kind toward his neighbors, rejecting any act of friendship he receives from them, being hostile and indifferent before the beauty of humanity, what do you think the problem might be?"

"It's very clear that this person has blocked off his zone of love creating an imbalance in the tetrahedron of the *to be* energy," Bruce responded with great confidence this time.

"Very well, and what do you all think will be the consequences of this imbalance?" asked Mester.

No one came forward to answer.

"In the answer to this question lies the answer to many of your questions. A malfunction in your *love* zone causes your bodies to grow sick."

A crowd of baffled expressions met Mester. Simon finally broke the silence. "So, you're saying that all sickness originates from a lack of love?"

"Exactly, as well as an excess of love. This is why one must be careful. In this world of polarity, no excess is good. It goes against the laws of Tellus, but these are not the true laws of creation. When you practice exaggerated love, you run the risk of losing or even forgetting about the love you owe yourself. Once this level is complete, the rules will change, and another level will commence with different rules that are much more coherent to your nature."

Mester was overjoyed when he realized that everyone seemed to understand his lesson thus far.

"See? This really is not so difficult. For now, observe the results of your actions to find the true origins of your problems. As you become skillful in this, you will be able to identify problems directly."

"What do we do about the sickness that consumes some of us?" a very old woman with a horrible cough asked.

"Identify the consequences of the problem and work on them. If they pertain to the *to be* energy, and your body is sick, open up your hearts and forgive. Follow your signs and wake up every morning with the faith that all your problems will be resolved, even if you don't know how yet. For those who have problems regarding the *to do* energy, silence your minds, slow down, and enjoy a beautiful sunset without worrying about the time. People lacking in this area will realize that time is their enemy."

Mester watched as the crowd slowly nodded in understanding.

"Well, I believe that this has been enough information for today," he said. "I'll be waiting here at the same time tomorrow to continue my teachings and clear any doubts you may have. May the Creator be with you."

The expressions of thanks created a sea of murmurs. Mester was thrilled that, for the first time, he had been able to relay some of the information that would change the destiny of the Telluranians.

The rest of the morning, everyone continued with their normal routines, even though Mester's parents knew there was no going back to normal. Mester had become a leader for the people of Tallen.

"Father, can I accompany you to your workshop? I would love to see how your creations take form." In fact, it reminded him with much nostalgia of someone he missed deeply.

Domino rested both hands over Mester's shoulders, "Of course, my son, but just know one thing: you are and always will be my best creation. Well, mine and your mother's," he gave Hazar a sideways glance and between laughs, they walked.

Domino's creations of wooden furniture were very popular among the people of Tallen. They were considered the most refined and elegant pieces of furniture, even among the upper class. The love with which he created these masterpieces, as well as his exquisite taste, made him duly prized among his customers. He charged significantly below the average price, and even though this sometimes led him to be taken advantage of, it mostly just helped him gain recognition within the town. His ultimate reward was the satisfaction he felt by making others happy.

Upon arriving at the workshop, he noticed something unusual.

"How strange. By this time, the workshop is usually packed with people waiting to put in their requests."

Recognizing the opportunity, Mester grabbed a pencil from Dominos ear with a naughty smile, took a piece of parchment he found on the floor and sat on a nearby tree trunk. His hands moved over the paper quickly, and with great expertise he produced a drawing, one Domino had never seen before.

"What are you drawing?" asked Domino in awe.

"It is a Merkaba; do you think that between us, we could build this?

Domino looked at the drawing. It was a complex figure heavily based on geometry, but even so, it did not appear to be too challenging to build.

"I don't know if this is by coincidence or not, but nobody came in today asking for anything, and that is very unusual. I think my intuition is telling me that it's you and your ideas I should focus on," he said in a joking manner.

"I see you're learning rather quickly," Mester flashed a witty smile.

The Creator of the Universe

"Well, time to get to work!" Domino shut the doors of the workshop and closed themselves off from the rest of the world.

The workshop was U-shaped, giving him a unique view from every direction around a colonnaded courtyard used to load and unload the merchandise. The ceilings were high, covered in palm leaves allowing the summer breeze to add a level of freshness to the work environment.

"Son, I think it's better that we build the Merkaba in the courtyard as it will be easier to move it out from here."

They were like two little kids building a rocket ship. Filling the workshop with laughter, they high-fiving each other every time they overcame a challenge. Mester's wisdom combined with Domino's manual skill meant that they accomplished a great deal very quickly.

The sunset brought along their first distraction: the grumbling in their stomachs. When they were finished, they stood back to admire the structure they had just built.

It was the work of supersonic art. Mester touched the Merkaba, tracing old memories with the Creator. He had been away for far too long.

"You have no idea how much this means to me, Father. Very soon, I will give you the details, but for now, I truly appreciate your help and your trust."

"Although I lack your wisdom, Mester, I know your heart and this is all I need to know."

They embraced each other and wiped off some of the sawdust that seemed to have taken a permanent hold on them.

"If your mother saw us like this, she would bathe us along with the donkeys," Domino said with a smile.

The small stubs of candles were the only source of light around the courtyard. Ready to leave, Domino blew out all the candles one by one. They waited for a darkness that never arrived. To their surprise, the courtyard remained illuminated by a faint golden light that brightened their faces. They looked up to the sky and noticed that just above the Merkaba, a golden light in the form of a tetrahedron had formed, making it look like a shining star.

"What is this? But, how? Mester, does this have something to do with the Merkaba?"

"Yes, Father, I am sorry. I had no idea how geometry would behave in this dimension." Mester anxiously stared at his father's face whose expression quite clearly painted the picture of bewilderment.

Soon, the silence of the night turned into voices of terror shouting, "Look! A sign from the sky!" As the seconds passed, the commotion of the people around the workshop grew, with crowds congregating in the streets in search of answers.

The effect of the light was so intense that it became a source of disturbance within the palace. The servants crowded the windows to watch. It looked like a human cocktail of confusion and surrealism.

King Aldon was enraged, for he could not stand a scenario of such great attraction that did not involve himself.

"What is this riot? Have you never seen the city of Tallen at night or what?" asked the king.

Helen, the chambermaid, nodded slowly. She kept her eyes down so as not to see his sour face.

"Yes ... but ... sorry your majesty, but do you not see those lights?" her trembling voice accompanied her whole body.

"What lights?"

"Those three golden lights in the shape of a pyramid?"

Aldon paused, assembling his thoughts.

"What kind of circus is this? Lights, pyramid. Sivilion! Go immediately and find out what is happening as well as what the people of the town are saying. Someone has to know something. Go!"

Sivilion scurried through the city. The footsteps of the king's cavalry was barely heard among the chaos of the crowd.

"Make way!" Sivilion shouted, who was absolutely disoriented because he was unable to see anything at all. Meanwhile, the people of the town seemed to be making their way just fine.

"Look! The star is right above Domino's workshop," shouted an old woman.

Domino felt a drum on his chest when he heard those words. "Mester, grab the blanket next to the wood-fired oven; let's cover the Merkaba before…" Mester seemed to understand exactly where his father was getting at because he was already doing so.

Between stumbles and scrapes, they covered the Merkaba, but to their dismay, it did not alter the light effect at all.

Domino rubbed his head in search of answers, "Mester, what should we do?"

Mester paused and suppressed his sigh "It's fine. Let's disassemble it," he said, dominated by a profound sadness.

Domino felt his heart break when he saw the sorrow on Mester's face as they dismantled the Merkaba. Though he knew it had to be done though, it was not worth risking their lives.

With the pieces already disassembled on the floor, an avalanche of blows knocked at the door.

"Open up. Show us what you have! In the name of Our Majesty, the King, open the door!"

The Creator of the Universe

Domino knew that Mester had never lied and would not start now. His body was frozen, "Come on, Mester. Let's go out the back door. You'll see them tomorrow. Come on, son!" Deep down, he was afraid he would not agree.

"Okay, but at some point, I'll have to talk."

"Oh, I almost forgot!" Domino grabbed Mester's drawing, folded it in two and put it in the pocket of his coat, pushing it to its deepest of depths. Losing that tiny paper would have been proof of the crime.

Silently, they left through the back door of the workshop and hid among the bushes. Seconds later, the crowd managed to force themselves through the front door. The soldiers' eyes looked like hunting dogs, but no prey seemed appetizing.

Walking home, the midnight blue canvas above stole every thought from their mind; the whirlwind of worries simply was forgotten. They looked into each other's eyes in a silent conversation that only left room for smiles. Mester felt as if they had just committed the worst of misdeeds, and the best part of it all was that his father was participating in it.

When they arrived home, Hazar was silent. She simply looked at them from head to toe. Domino's skin had layers of sawdust and his hair could have been confused for snow.

"What horror, Domino! Are you all right? In all our years of marriage, I have never seen you in such a condition!"

"Is this the *to do* energy speaking?" Domino asked as he clutched his stomach from the pain of laughing.

"I don't find this amusing. I thought something had happened to you both. I should make you go shower with the donkeys, but I will let this one go. Step into the shower, I will bring you both some hot water."

Hazar was upset, but even that did not seem to wash away the happiness from Domino and Mester's expressions.

The Creator of the Universe

Whenever they looked at each other, they were like two kids bonding under the scornful gaze of a mother.

During dinner, they filled Hazar in on the adventures of the day and explained to her what they had built. Domino took Mester's drawing from his coat and proudly showed it to her. Neither one intended to talk about their recent events, at least not for the time being.

Hazar raised her hands to cover the shock on her face. Her gaze grew sad, and her breaths shortened. Domino and Mester exchanged glances, worried that she might know something about what had happened at the workshop.

"Are you alright, Mother? Don't you like it?"

"No, son, it's not that. Would you believe me if I told you this isn't the first time I've seen this?"

"Seen what? The Merkaba?" Waiting for her to clarify.

"Yes".

Domino now looked as surprised as ever. "Where could you possibly have seen this structure before?

I've seen this many times in my dreams."

"What's so bad about that, Hazar?" He asked with some relief.

"What's bad is that in my dream, Mester is inside this thing and it takes him further and further away from us. I am not there with him. It scares me." Hazar began to sob.

Mester immediately understood his mother's intuition and hugged her tightly, assuring her that he would never leave her.

"Mother, please do not fear. Do not tie yourself to the nonexistent reality of this world. Trust me when I tell you that this other place to which we are headed is much better. All you have to do is make sure you live a good life in this world, so you can enter an even better one."

Mester's words gave her some comfort. She wanted to believe it was so, but could not stop her thoughts from wavering back to her dreams. She had tried to bury them in the deepest part of her mind, but one way or another they were determined to resurface.

"Son, why do you always talk about what we have to do, but you never include yourself? Are you not coming with us when we go to this better world?"

This question made every neuron in Mester's brain work at the speed of light. "We will find each other again, just in different times. Do not worry, Mother. Have faith for now."

Always trying to alleviate any tension in the room, Domino said, "I have an idea. Let's all get to bed to be ready for tomorrow. Who knows? Maybe it'll be all three of us who get on that spaceship and go for a little ride."

"You and your jokes." A little smile formed at the corners of Hazar's mouth.

It had been a long day, and exhaustion took hold of them, except for Hazar, who evaded sleep for as long as possible to avoid that reoccurring dream.

As the sun rose, excitement rushed back into Mester. Domino awoke in search of Hazar, whom he found sitting on the sofa, her head tilted sideways and her glasses halfway down her nose. "Hazar! My love! Are you all right? You fell asleep here. Why didn't you go to bed?"

Hazar did not want to answer and changed the topic. "You both go to the river. I am tired. By the time you come back, I should feel better."

Domino knew she was hiding something. He kissed her on the forehead and covered her with her favorite blanket hoping to bring her some comfort. As Domino passed by the dining room table, his eyes clung onto the Merkaba drawing lying on the table. He did not need any more reminders rolling that could torment Hazar so he grabbed it, placing it neatly in the pocket of his coat.

The Creator of the Universe

Soon enough, Hazar heard a door open and shut, and its creaking noise brought a chill to her spine. Her tears burst forth like water from a dam, spilling down her face.

On their walk to the river, Domino asked Mester, "What were you planning to do with the Merkaba?"

"As soon as I had covered all my points, I was going to use it to put my theory into practice." The sigh that escaped from his lips was slow. However, his eyes flung wide, soaring to new heights of emotions when he saw the number in the crowd awaiting him. The cheers erupted like a volcano.

"My dear Mester, what a pleasure it is to meet you. I have heard great things about you. My name is Luz. I am Pastor Joel's sister and, if you will accept me, I would love to hear you speak." She was an old woman, worn and frail.

"You, along with anyone else who wishes to come, will always be welcome." He took her hand and guided her to the roots of an ancient cedar tree, where she might be comfortable as he spoke.

"Mester, do you have any idea about what happened yesterday? We all saw a light in the form of a pyramid whose center was located just above your father's workshop," said Luz as her eyebrows curled.

"Not everyone did," interrupted Bruce. "That phenomenon was not seen by all. King Aldon and his squadron were roaming around for hours and could not see anything. What really happened? How do you explain that some saw it and others did not?"

"We cannot all see the same things. It becomes impossible to see beyond what we are not. It is an issue of evolution that entails a process." Mester looked at his father in an uneasy manner, and quickly changed the subject.

"I will continue yesterday's lecture, and for those of you who have come for the first time, I will stay a while longer at the end to explain what you have missed."

"Mester, I'm sorry, but I don't have much money to pay. How much will these lessons cost?" asked the elderly woman.

"My dear Madam Luz, charging you for my teachings would be like a parent charging his children for raising them. Would you do that? Charge someone who brings so much joy to your life?"

"Of course not! That would be absurd!" cried the audience.

"It's not all that absurd. What you give from the heart you cannot sell, and if you sell it, then it is not from the heart. Here is your fifth lesson: judgment. Quite often, you find yourselves in difficult situations, and it is precisely in these moments that the most difficult decisions must be made. Your intuition always tells you the right direction to take, but it can be hard to hear among the million excuses and possible outcomes. Not listening to your intuition is like fishing with the best fishing rod, in the best boat, and on the best of water without a hook. Your *to be* energy is never confused and can decipher what is true from what is false to always choose the right path. Any decision guided by reason or the *to do* energy, without approval from the heart or the *to be* energy, will be destined for failure."

"How does your heart know what the right decision is?" asked Bruce.

"Here, on Tellus, there are three forms of time: past, present, and future. These three zones are only perceptions of time, which does not actually exist. The reality is that these zones occur simultaneously, and you have already lived your future, even though your *to do* does not remember. However, your intuition or *to be* does recall this."

"Now, I really feel as if I've learned nothing in school," sighed Bruce, rubbing his head to relieve the headache he felt coming. "How is this possible? What is the point? How do we prove that time doesn't exist?"

The Creator of the Universe

"When you eat an apple, do you analyze and prove its biological process? Or do you simply eat it and enjoy it?" Mester asked.

"I simply eat it."

"Then why not enjoy this new information, and later you can attempt to prove it?"

"I'm sorry, Mester, but my confusion is just too great. You're suddenly telling me that everything I have learned is no longer useful."

"I understand Bruce, but why don't you try to gain some insight, and observe me — even with your doubts. Focus on all past and future points that I will show you. Let the information of wisdom flow within you without resisting, and you can then draw your own conclusions based on your personal experience. How are you to say that the apple you are eating is the best one of them all if you have not tried others? To make good use of your insight, we must increase our wisdom. Without it, there is no moving forward."

The sea of lost eyes reflected the crowd's thoughts, as they began to accept Mester's words. It was as if they were beginning to remember something they already knew.

"What happens if you make the wrong decision?" asked Luz, who seemed very concerned. "I mean, how are we supposed to apply all this new information without making a mistake?"

"At no point in my lesson did I correlate a mistake with failure. Yes, you will not always make the wisest choices, but such choices are not mistakes. It all depends on how you look at it, leading us to our sixth point: Your knowledge weeps at your mistakes; however, your wisdom learns from them."

Mester paced for a few moments, collecting his thoughts before continuing. "When knowledge fails, it is your ego that loses the battle, creating a sequence of signs and critiques that ultimately destroy your *to do*. When you make a mistake, allow your heart to assure and explain to you where you went wrong and give you all possible solutions. *To be* mistakes are not failures. They are simply lessons in your book of personal wisdom."

"What happens when we make a mistake and others laugh and humiliate us just because we may not be as smart as they are? How are we to ignore them?" Bruce attempted to mask the pain in his voice.

"Brothers and sisters, when someone offends you and hurts your feelings, is it really their fault? Or is it yours for allowing them to make you feel that way?" Mester asked.

"It is their fault because my ears can listen to their insults and that hurts." This time the pain in Bruce's voice was more evident.

"Believe it or not, it is ultimately your fault. When there is an act of aggression toward you and you have a negative reaction toward it, it creates a duality of sorts because of the great tension between two opposites. However, if you give no reaction to these insults, the conflict has nothing to thrive on, weakening this tension. When you are insulted, your *to be* should respond by rejecting insults. For example, do you let strangers into your homes?"

"Of course not!" they yelled.

"Well, you're *to be* is your home and an overprotective parent, making sure no harm comes to your spiritual fortress. Moving on to my seventh point: An opposition feeds opposing forces, while a lack of a reaction weakens them."

A homeless man without a spark of expression on his face interrupted. "Why do good and bad have to exist? Wouldn't it be better if we were all good and loved each other unconditionally? Why do we have to suffer? Why are there people who are rich and people who are poor? Why is there happiness and sadness? If this Creator you speak of is as great as you say, why did he create all of this?"

The Creator of the Universe

Mester felt as if his lungs had forgotten how to breathe, and the color drained from his face at the thought of people accusing the Creator for YinYang's actions. "What's your name, my brother?"

"Juan."

"Juan, I see a lot of pain in your expression and a great emptiness in your heart."

"Does losing my wife and children to illness count as sadness? If the Creator is so great, may he return them to me?" He yelled, releasing years of pent-up anger.

Mester moved to embrace Juan, whose entire body screamed agony in its purest form. He had never seen someone in such torment. He knew that nothing he said would be enough because the man's zone of faith was completely blocked. He had to help this man.

"Juan, when I have finished all my lessons, I invite you to travel to heaven. When you see it, you will understand just how wrong your perspective is. Let me give you an example. You are in a war zone and people die. They kill each other and starve. However, someone comes and offers to take your wife and children to a paradise full of flowers, food, and harmony, free of illness and suffering. Would you let them go or would you want them with you?"

Juan looked at him, confused. "Despite the great pain of their absence, I would want them in a safer place."

"Very well. What makes you think that they aren't?"

"I can't see them. I know nothing. How am I supposed to know they are alright?"

"Juan, your faith is so weak that I will show you this place to help you, but after, you must put forth great effort to believe without proof. I am not telling you to believe in everything anyone tells you, but to believe based on your intuition and your capacity to judge. Tomorrow, I will give you all the last four lessons, and after that, I will show you heaven, Juan."

Juan's faith had floated away from him a very long time ago, like a leaf being drowned into a deep ocean, but Mester's words shined bright like a star in his hopelessly dark universe.

"I think that is enough for today," Mester said in respect for Juan's pain. "Many of you have lessons to practice, and I ask for your patience."

One by one, they approached Mester, thanking him. The happiness soaking their faces was all the reward Mester needed.

On their way back, Domino asked Mester, "How do you intend to show heaven to Juan without the Merkaba?"

"I do not know father, but my intuition made me say it so let's have faith." He kept his eyes up with his mind tuned into a positive thought.

When Bruce arrived at work, everyone noticed that his behavior was much different from usual. He did not yell or raise his voice in the slightest to his employees and his eyes were filled with a newfound kindness. Eventually, gossip reached the ears of King Aldon, who called for Bruce immediately.

"I have heard that you have lost respect before your subordinates. They say you have turned soft and thoughtful. Is this true?"

"I do not understand what you are referring to, Your Highness." Bruce cleared his throat, not realizing the impact that Mester had made on him. For the first time in forever, his body and mind relaxed.

"I'm giving you fair warning. To control the mass of people that we do, you must do it with superiority. If you show consideration, they will ask you for a raise, which leads to wanting education and better conditions."

"But, Your Highness, what is so wrong in that?" asked Bruce.

"You don't understand how power works, Bruce. If most of the people can obtain an education and food, it would become very difficult to control them."

"But, if they were educated, there wouldn't be so many wars, which, in turn, leads to higher levels of consciousness that lower the risk of the destruction of the human race."

"What is going on with you, Bruce? Consciousness is of no interest to me. I want power—that is it! You better understand this, or I will have no consideration for you." King Aldon answered with such sternness that the words echoed in Bruce's mind.

"Yes, Your Highness." Bruce kept his eyes down to hide his disagreement.

King Aldon was surprised by this sudden change in Bruce, being fully aware that this was not the man he hired.

"I'm not sure what's happened to you, Bruce, but I suggest you snap out of it." It worried him that his right-hand man, the man who managed his entire fortune, could have undergone such a drastic change of heart. "You're dismissed."

Once Bruce shuffled away, King Aldon called for Sivilion, army general, as well as his shadow. "Follow Bruce day and night and inform me immediately of anything you find."

Sivilion bowed as a sign of inferiority and began his hunt.

When Domino and Mester returned home, they were surprised by the smell of roasted lamb, the rich aroma of the dish wafted all over the house. Domino knew Hazar must have been feeling better, since she only cooked that dish for special occasions.

"My love, it smells delightful! What calls for this celebration?"

"Nothing really, I just want to celebrate that I have you both here with me right now, despite what tomorrow may bring," Hazar responded with unusual calmness.

Domino had never heard Hazar talk in such a nonchalant manner. Although it surprised him, he was happy to see this new attitude in her.

The huge mahogany dining table perfectly varnished shined, reflecting the beautiful decoration above the table. At its center, one tall, silver vase full of flowers commanded attention, surrounded by acacia wooden platters marked by Domino's fingerprints on it.

If they could have opened their mouth any wider they would have eaten the whole lamb in one bite. As if in a hypnotic trance, their hands moved forward ready to grab a piece, "Nuh Uh! First, wash your hands, the food won't move from here," Hazar winked at them.

After following instructions, they all hurried to the table. Holding hands, they were saying grace when a great knock on the door interrupted.

"I'll get it!" said Mester.

"Juan! What a wonderful surprise."

"I'm sorry for the interruption, but I followed you here to make sure you wouldn't disappear on me, seeing as you're my only hope."

"Please, come inside, food is served. Please join us." Mester understood exactly why he was worried.

"If you just serve me the food, I can eat outside as I always do." Juan did not dare to enter. From the door, he could see the table beautifully arranged, and in no way did he feel worthy.

"What do you mean 'outside'? You, my father, my mother, and I are all equals. The difference only exists in your mind, not ours. For us, it is an honor to have you here. Plus, this way you'll be able to keep a closer eye on me,"

Mester said, hoping to get a smile out of the man. He took Juan by the arm and sat him firmly in a chair.

Juan smiled. He had never witnessed this much kindness. For a moment, everyone forgot about etiquette. Juan was licking his fingers, smeared with sauce and oil and with the intention of making him feel at home, the rest did the same. A meal that had taken Hazar hours to prepare was gone in a matter of minutes, but the company had made it worthwhile.

Time, as always, interrupted the moment. Hazar's mother antique clock chimed, waking Domino from what seemed like a beautiful dream.

"It's already 2 o'clock! "I almost forgot—I must return to the workshop and finish Bruce's order."

"If you would allow me, I would like to help you. That way, I can repay you in some way for this beautiful gesture," Juan said.

"Of course you can accompany me, my friend, but not to repay me, just for enjoyment," Domino responded in his usual generous manner.

Mester stayed behind with Hazar to help her clean the table and wash the dishes.

"Mother, I want to thank you for this delicious meal, but if you don't mind me saying, you added too much, as always, of one ingredient."

"Oh no, really? Was it too salty?" asked Hazar with disappointment.

"No, no, Mother! It just had a lot of love." Mester giggled.

"You and your jokes. You're just like your father."

"That's not a bad thing. When your spirit is happy, you cannot contain it. It's like a blooming flower, too beautiful to cut it."

The Creator of the Universe

Hazar looked at her son with tenderness. "You're right. I suppose I should try to stop cutting flowers for the table."

Mester burst out laughing. For the first time, he had actually witnessed his mother making a joke.

They spent the rest of the afternoon laughing like never before. When Domino returned home, for a second he thought he had walked into the wrong house. He had never heard his wife laugh so much. Without difficulty, Domino added himself into the conversation, along with another layer of happiness.

"Father, how is Juan? Has he come with you?"

"I had no idea that Juan was also a carpenter. Had it not been for his help, I would not have finished Bruce's order so quickly. I offered him a place to sleep in the workshop. Although it embarrassed him, he accepted. He is a good man."

"Thank you for your great kindness, Father. The universe will repay you somehow. This will be one of my lectures tomorrow. Mother, please do not miss the meeting. I need you both there. My message must transcend generations until Tellus can lift the veil from its eyes. The Creator does not want the truth to be hidden from you. None of you deserve this." YinYang slipped back into Mester's thoughts as he went to bed.

Both Domino and Hazar realized that when Mester referred to the problems that the Telluranians faced, he lost his composure. Apparently, this was the only topic that caused him discomfort.

The next morning black clouds sprawled across the sky. A lightning boom rolled across the valley, announcing the start of what the brooding cloud layer had promised since dawn.

The Creator of the Universe

Domino was somewhat impatient. He kept looking out the window, but the sun gave no sign of making an appearance.

"Hazar, if this rain continues, we will be unable to take even a single step outside. I will go to the workshop to grab the carriage and some blankets. I'll be back soon."

He searched for his coat but could not find it. "I must have left my coat at the workshop."

"Put this jacket on and take my umbrella. It's a bit feminine but with this rain you will not notice it." Laughter shook them to the door.

Domino stepped outside and after a few experimental drops, the clouds unleashed a torrent of water. The drops struck the already wet sidewalk, pitting the surface as if they were bullets falling from the sky.

Domino arrived to the workshop completely soaked. He sat down and removed his shoes and socks to try to warm himself up. Taking a rest from the wet battle his mind got back on track. "Juan are you here?" He quickly glanced around for Juan, but his breath cut short when his gaze reached the back of the shop. There it was, the Merkaba, exactly the way he had remembered it.

"How was it assembled? What happened?" In the midst of so many questions, Juan's face appeared, his facial expression signaled he had something to do with it.

"Sir I am sorry. I only wanted to help. I got up early and could not go back to sleep because of the thunder, so I started to organize the workshop. When I took your coat to place it over your chair to make sure it did not get wet, a picture fell out of the pocket. I found it a bit strange, but very simple to assemble since the pieces were already cut. But if you want me to, I can take it apart right now?"

"Umm...No...No, Juan, it's fine. You did good." He did not have the heart to tell him to dismantle the Merkaba, he knew how much it meant to Mester.

He noticed that the Merkaba was still illuminated but it no longer had the same light effect as last time since it was now daytime. *This could not have been planned any better. What a masterful way of synchronizing events. This is definitely a sign. When Mester sees this...*

Mester was ready with his nose crushed against the window, making sure to be the first one to notice Domino's arrival.

"Do you really think all those people will be waiting at the river for you in this weather?" asked Hazar.

"When we most want something in life is when we encounter the most obstacles. These tests make us realize how much we truly want something and how willing we are to meet those challenges to achieve our goals." Mester spoke with assurance. "Despite the rain, I will go because I came to Tellus to teach you the truth. If the others are there in this storm, it's because what I have taught them has reached the wisdom in their hearts as opposed to the *to do*, which will advise them to stay home."

Hazar listened to Mester without saying a single word. Rummaging through an old trunk beside her bed, she shook out two dusty and wrinkled raincoats. "Put these on, and don't worry about the dust, they're about to get a wash." Once again, laughter commenced, mixed in with the smell of coffee. "Sit down for breakfast. Today will be a rather long day."

A few minutes later, the galloping sound of the horses against the cobblestone streets announced Domino's arrival. With one jump, Mester made his way to the exit, he took the raincoat and between sneezes from the dust, he broke into a run.

"Good morning, Mester," Domino called out as he reined the horse to a halt. "I don't think it's a good day to walk. What do you say you all accompany me, seeing that

The Creator of the Universe

this carriage is rather uncomfortable when it's empty...well, except in the back!"

Mester's eyes lit up, "Is that the Merkaba?"

"The universe has an interesting way of working things out. This one we owe to Juan." Domino replied with a wink.

"Mother, hurry! I told you it was going to be a grand day! The universe always has a way of making things work out when it comes to the universal order," Mester squealed as he hauled himself into the carriage.

"A universal order?" Hazar whispered under the rain. "I may have given birth to this son of mine, but sometimes I truly don't understand him."

The diffused grey light of a darkening sky pushed light just far enough to see figures silhouetted by the river. A spark of hope ran through Mester's veins. They stopped the carriage right under the cedar in hopes of gaining some shelter under the leafy branches. Already, a great number of people had shown up, and Mester watched them trying to remember those who had been there the day before. Only a few people were familiar, since the number of the audience had tripled.

Mester approached the crowd as the first ray of light hit them and the grey skies began to break. "Mester, do you also control the weather? How did you make the rain stop? What more are you capable of?" some people yelled.

"Brothers and sisters, do not misinterpret what just happened. I did not make the rain stop. What just happened was a test for you all. How many of you doubted whether you should come today when you awoke to a storm?"

Just about everyone raised their hands.

"Now, tell me why you all have come today."

"Honestly, I'm not entirely sure. There was something telling me to come even though I thought I was partially insane for wanting to step out into that storm," Madam Luz blurted.

"Me too! Me too!" The whole crowd agreed.

"Good. That something telling you to come today was your intuition, the only part of you that knows what is best. I'm very pleased to see that you are all learning to live your lives based on your intuition. It will not always be easy. Sometimes your intuition might seem defective, but there will always be a reason for everything it tells you, even if you do not understand. My eighth lesson is that to believe is to bring your creations to life. The universe favors dreamers with discipline."

"You were all made to be free, to dream and to elevate your imagination with no limits. Nevertheless, your fear of failure holds you down and stops you from moving forward. What do you have to lose by trying to achieve a dream? The worst that could happen is that your attempt does not work on the first try, but you learn from it, pick yourself back up, and try again. You will see the importance of perseverance. You won't know when your attempts will be successful, but what is certain is that a time will come when you will obtain great wisdom, and your knowledge will be enslaved by that wisdom."

"I have seen people who have great dreams and work very hard, but they are never acknowledged. They never achieve fame," a new voice said.

"Dear friend, what is your name?"

"My name is Omar, but people call me Bad Luck." The man appeared to be bored and was slurring his words. His height further accentuated the curvature of his back, making him seem much older.

"If I may ask, of the things you have done in life, have you done them in hopes of seeking fame and the recognition of others?"

"No, I was speaking about other people, not of myself!" he quickly responded.

"Let's use you for an example then." Mester knew he needed to get past Omar's ego.

"Well...I would like the recognition."

"Then, it's safe to say that you are not after a dream. You are looking for a way to satisfy your ego. When you go chasing your dreams, the only person's approval you should seek is your own. Let me share with you an example. One day, you decide to write a book, and you put in your best effort. You enjoy it and spend hours on it, and time seems to lose its effect. When you finally awaken from this long trance, you realize that you have completed your work of art—a work that brought you much happiness and spiritual fulfillment. In that moment, you have achieved your dream. You managed to put on paper a part of yourself. Now, people read it and identify with your book. Surely, it will be sold in many different languages, and you will become famous! If you look closely, in the first phase you achieved your dream, and in the second, you became famous. However, what makes you think that in the first stage you were not successful? Your ego, searches for the approval of others. When this happens, the universe stops helping you."

"You mean I have no right to sell something I made?"

"If you want fame, make business deals. If you want success, dream." Mester gently placed his hand on Omar's shoulder.

Omar understood Mester's words perfectly, but something was still bothering him. This time, he spoke in first person. "I try to do things right, but they always turn out wrong. That is why they call me Bad Luck."

"When things don't go your way, you simply have to change your way of doing things and be more flexible. If you allow criticism to affect you, it will take away from the energy you could be focusing on something more useful. Confront these obstacles with serenity, learn from them, and overcome them." He offered Omar a reassuring smile.

"When I asked you what your name was, you said 'Omar, but people call me Bad Luck.' You gave importance to what others call you. I only asked for your name. You must look deeper inside yourself, Omar. Tell yourself every day how happy you are with what you have achieved. What others think about you is their problem, not yours. You have paid a great price to make what others see in you your reality. It's time to take back control of your life."

"Thank you, Mester." Omar struggled to speak, and from his expression, it was evident that Mester's words had hit home.

"Our ninth lesson is to look for the beauty in the spirit. Look at your surroundings. You see an abundance of beautiful creations—the cedar tree that gives us shade, the river reflecting every shade of blue, and the green meadow feeding our sheep. Appreciating this beauty is necessary for your spiritual evolution. Unfortunately, in Tellus, beauty and what is good do not go hand in hand. What is beautiful is not necessarily good. What is good is not necessarily beautiful. When one has physical beauty, you must put forth great effort to look beyond artificial beauty until you find the beauty that grows within and radiates outward without control. Only when you have achieved this, will you have achieved your true purpose in this world. You must see beyond what your eyes show you."

"What happens to the elderly who are ugly like me?" interrupted Madam Luz. "Can we really radiate beauty?"

"My dear lady, everyone has a special gift that helps them achieve their maximum potential. For those who do not display physical beauty, there is a greater need to work on your interior to develop your potential. As your inner beauty exceeds its capacity, it begins to radiate in a physical sense, in a way that never grows old. Being physically beautiful can open many doors for you in this world, but this is not what you came here for. You are all here to achieve spiritual beauty, despite your challenges."

"What can we do after this life with spiritual beauty?"

"The same things you would do after obtaining the knowledge of mathematics! Do long and complex equations. This is only the first step—better said, it's the entry ticket to a more advanced school, where what is good and what is beautiful are at last one."

"Why teach us first that what is good and what is beautiful are separate and then later tell us they're one? Wouldn't it be better to learn from the start how things really are?" asked Bruce, utterly confused.

For the third time now, Mester was forced into silence. "Yes, it would be better, but that is not something we can change. For now, you should focus on overcoming challenges and not questioning them. Otherwise, you risk entering a labyrinth with no exit. Have patience. For now, only your love, faith, and intuition can guide you to the truth."

"What is the next level?" many people asked.

"It's a level with greater coherence, but we'll talk about it later, after Juan accompanies me to heaven. He will be the one to describe this place to you."

Juan's heart beat so fast that it made his chest sore. He finally felt like someone understood his pain. He did not know what would happen next, the only thing he did know was that Mester's promises had rekindled his hope.

Mester noticed that Juan had a different air about him. His face was no longer dirty and his attire was clean and very familiar.

Suddenly, a child interrupted. "Am I pretty or ugly, Mester?" His laughter was contagious, and it actually reminded him of Kozma. He was German's son, the town baker, well known for his elaborate wedding cakes.

"Excuse my son. I didn't have anyone to leave him with, and my wife had an errand to run." German was extremely embarrassed by the boy's interruption.

"Don't be embarrassed, German. I love children. They are noble, sincere, and pure. I actually meant to make a point about them, so I'm glad you reminded me."

"My name is Mateo." The boy interrupted again.

"Mateo, the beauty of children is authentic, and you say what you think or feel directly from your *to be*. Unfortunately, as you continue to grow, you will begin to lose that clarity. To a certain extent, you will all become contaminated with the beliefs imposed on you or your *to do*."

"Then, I don't want to grow up!" yelled Mateo. Their joyful laughter could be heard from a mile away.

"Do not worry, Mateo. Life on Tellus is a cycle. You are born knowing. You grow up in ignorance, and when you get older, you retrieve your knowledge."

"So, you mean that Madam Ana and I are the only ones who know?"

"Something like that," Mester responded, barely able to contain his laughter.

Without wasting time, Mateo asked, "Then why do you know so much if you're neither a child nor an elder? Who are you? Where do you come from? You're not from here, right?"

Mester could sense great evolution in Mateo, but answering his questions would be getting ahead of himself, for many people would not be ready to hear what he had to say. "Little by little, I will explain it all to you, Mateo. For now, you will have to have patience."

"Yes, sir," Mateo breathed in deeply with resignation. He was a very bright boy, but he was also a very respectful one. His father had been careful to teach Mateo how to put his gifts to good use, without sacrificing his inner self.

The Creator of the Universe

"If there are no other questions, we will move on to lesson number ten: Your mission is to love and restore the interrupted wisdom. It might seem very simple to you, but this is the most important lesson. Despite the duality of the world in which you live, you are all free to pick your own path. When you chose to live in love by rejecting hate, you send a message to the cosmos that you chose the path of civilization, which frees you and restores the cosmic order."

"Frees us from what?" asked German.

Mester decided it was time. Uncomfortable, he said, "Freeing you from an unjust situation, in which the laws of the universe weren't applied correctly."

"You mean to say we are a mistake of the universe?" Domino asked.

"No! Nothing that comes from the Creator is a mistake. There can be a momentary imbalance or disorder, but ultimately the essence of creation is that love will always return to its origin."

"Why was an imbalance produced?"

"It's important that you don't question 'why' instead of 'what for.' The 'why' distracts you from your true purpose. Asking 'what for' shows the universe that you forgive the injustices you encounter. Great acts of love show this forgiveness, allowing you to enter a superior level and reestablishing the order that belong to you."

"If it belongs to us, who took it away?" asked German in great worry.

"German, you know your son is very talented, right?" German lowered his head humbly.

"Let's suppose that one day you decide to trust your son to make one of your famous cakes for a very important client. What would you do if Mateo's cake did not come out right? Would you blame him? Or would you take responsibility along with your son and try to fix the damage?"

"I would assume responsibility. He is my son, and I am responsible for his actions."

"That's exactly how great the Creator's love is for you. He allowed me to come here to help his children repair the damage."

"Then it was someone's error!" exclaimed German.

"It wasn't someone's error; it was a mistake. An error is unfixable, unlike a mistake that can be fixed with forgiveness. Forgiveness will make you worthy of a place within the cosmic nature that awaits you so graciously."

"So, you're saying an error and a mistake aren't the same?"

"When you make an error, you understand something as wrong and aimless. On the other hand, the word mistake refers to a division between two paths of equal force. In contrast to errors, mistakes allow you to reverse the damage done by taking the correct path and straightening things out."

Everyone looked at one another, confused. Speaking of errors and mistakes had not been the best idea, so Mester quickly changed the subject and mentioned his last lesson.

"The last and eleventh lesson is healing through forgiveness. Negative emotions, like hate, jealousy, and resentment, do not belong to your essence. When you host these emotions for too long, your body identifies them and quickly drives them out through illness. In this way, illness is a detoxification process for your body."

"How can we cure ourselves if the body has to detoxify?" asked Juan with great interest.

"You must first identify the problem, making a very heartfelt and honest evaluation from your heart to recognize situations in which you have failed. The moment you let a feeling or thought outside of your nature enter, you become responsible for it and you are the only one capable of reversing it."

"In my case, life took away my loved ones. How do I not feel hate?"

"Your case, Juan, is a little more complex. It is not about someone doing something to you. It is about the unawareness of what is real. You think that something bad happened to them, when it was actually the complete opposite. Later, you will understand what I speak of." Mester placed his hands over his shoulders to reassure him.

From the multitudes of people emerged a homeless woman named Alma. Her face was covered with old draping, and Mester could barely make out what she asked. He moved toward her to better understand her words.

"What happens if–if I have caused much harm to someone and after I apologize, she refuses to forgive me?" She bowed her head with much embarrassment.

"My beautiful Alma, I imagine you have paid quite heavily for your action, to such a point that you feel as if you can't escape your conscience until you have received this person's forgiveness." Her eyes dripped with tears. "From now on, you must come to the realization that once you have asked for forgiveness sincerely, the universe will hear you and acknowledge your regret. Whether the person forgives or not is out of your control. Continuing to seek and beg for her forgiveness will only bring you worse disappointments. You must forgive yourself by making up for your mistakes with good actions—this is the true state of forgiveness. Even though forgiveness from others serves as a painkiller for your soul, it is not imperative." Mester's words were the release valve she had been in need of for so long.

"Mester, could you speak more about healing?" Bruce could not wait any longer. His wife had not been feeling well lately, and he wanted to find a way to help her.

"The first day I spoke to you all about the six energetic points, three in the *to do* and three in the *to be*, formed by the two tetrahedron. The *to be* pyramid pointing upward

The Creator of the Universe

consists of love, intuition, and faith, while the *to do* pyramid pointing downward consists of the brain, body, and action. Each one of these is represented by a different color.

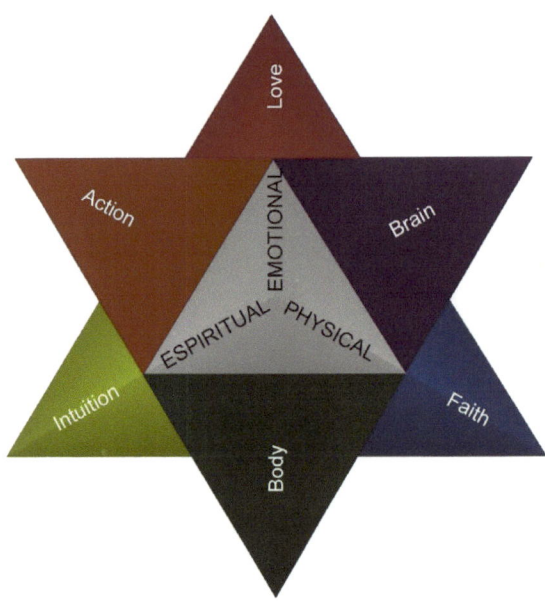

"Love, which is represented by the color red, is the energy that controls your emotions. Love is a catalyst for emotional information, calibrated to the source of creation. It helps you learn by contrast. Any excess—or lack of love creates an imbalance within the *to be* pyramid's foundation."

"Intuition is represented by the color yellow. This energy is like the reins of a horse—it controls the way to your destiny. Excess use of intuition compromises your brain, creating an imbalance, but failing to use it will cause you to wander with no true direction. Every element is directly related to another, and no element is more important than the next—at least this is true here in Tellus."

The Creator of the Universe

"Faith is represented by the color blue. This energy is a catalyst for your intuition. When your intuition indicates which path to take, the path does not exist in your reality. You co-create this path from nothing with the help of your faith. Faith is the greatest architect of your reality on Tellus.

"The brain takes the color purple and processes information, allowing for fluid shifts of this information. Unlike your intuition, the brain knows exact geographic coordinates of information, even when your destiny may not be clear. A balance between your brain and intuition further amplifies its performance, bringing together your unconscious wisdom with your conscious knowledge.

"Action is represented by the color orange and is a vibrant energy that opens up pathways to the creation with faith. Action is the force of the horses that drive you to move forward, but without faith, the scope of the achievement would be limited."

"The body is represented by the color green and is the materialized expression of your spirit. It works like a projector, showing both good and bad functionality of your inner self. When your spirit is not working properly, it is immediately released from the body through illness. It is important that you understand the link between love and the body because these two energetic points are directly correlated. When you feel an excess of love for someone, you run the risk of forgetting about yourself or placing your happiness in something unstable. In addition, if you feel too much hatred or resentment, the spirit tries to release itself from the grip of this negative energy by directing it toward the body. In both cases, imbalance is harmful, and the only way to create a sane body is to control your emotions."

"Also, your body is an energetic point of sex. This is the most powerful energy of creation within your reach. If this energy is capable of creating other lives, imagine what you all would be capable of achieving in your lives if this energy were used correctly."

No one knew how to react. Many redirected their line of sight to Pastor Joel.

"I truly don't understand anything!" The Pastor paused to gather his thoughts. "You're saying that having sex is good, my son?"

"Pastor Joel, you shouldn't see sex as something strange or secretive. After all, aren't all Telluranians created through sex? Problems occur in how it is used. When this act is consumed between two individuals who are connected on an emotional level, a sexual magic is created that is not only capable of creating life, but also of bringing to life desires on this plane. You are all part of the Creator, and if he has the ability to create, then so do you. This is why love is the key that opens the door to sexual acts."

The pastor rubbed at the goosebumps on his skin. "What about people who are, well, a bit generous with sexual acts?" The pastor was not used to discussing this matter so openly.

"Pastor, do not fret." Mester was actually growing concerned that this man was about to have a heart attack. "They have sexual relations with no emotional connection. In those cases, no magic occurs. It is quite the opposite actually. What happens is a draining of the physical field, and that energy is ultimately lost."

"And what happens to those like me, who do not engage in sexual relations?"

"Don't worry. In some cases, when your profession or physical condition does not allow for it, devotion or sacrifice is transmitted into energy for humanity and the greater good. You all receive the benefits, but those who pursue sexual relations in honest ways should make use of this gift and be grateful that the universe has placed it in your hands."

Domino and Hazar looked at each other questioningly. They both knew these topics had never been discussed at home.

The temperature of the meeting place rose, and in hopes of easing the tensions a little, Bruce interrupted, "Once problems arrive, how are we to know what it is that we lack?"

"You will all be presented with three types of challenges here on Tellus based on your emotional, physical, and spiritual zones. When your body becomes sick, review the energy of love, which will have been affected to a certain degree. When the reality you are co-creating for yourself is no longer what you want it to be, analyze your actions and decide if they align with that which you desire. Finally, when you are not clear on your own personal goals or not capable of answering why you are here on Tellus, listen to your intuition and silence your brain.

Imagine that every one of the elements that I just explained is an all-important part of a carriage. Here, emotional energy is the horse's food, physical energy is the motor power of the horses to move the carriage, and spiritual energy is the horse's reins. These energies are equally important to the success of your journey."

Mester's smile suddenly turned into a sly one as he made eye contact with Juan. Struggling to contain his excitement, he removed the old rags covering the structure that Juan had just reconstructed.

"Mester, what is that thing?"

"What took you all so long to ask, Juan?" He giggled. "It's called the Merkaba, a vehicle used to ascend. The true Merkaba is not made of wood. This is just an example. The Merkaba is an energetic field, with a geometric shape like the one you see here, but it is not visible. This is just to help you visualize it. You must learn to control your deceitful eyes. Do not wait to see. You must feel it."

"What happens when all these energetic points work perfectly?"

"The pyramid pointing upward rotates in a clockwise direction, while the opposite pyramid rotates in a counterclockwise manner. When these two forces manage to rotate at equal intensity in opposite directions, the movement of your energetic field becomes fluid, facilitating your experience here on Tellus and guaranteeing a shift to a superior level. Once you learn to control it, you will no longer have to return to Tellus after death because you have nothing left to learn here."

"What happens with the Merkaba when we achieve the next level?"

"The Merkaba will only serve as a way to leave this level because once there, the laws of geometry change."

"What are the following laws of geometry?"

"The cube, but for now, only focus on the Merkaba. What is important is what you achieve within this plane."

Sivilion hid among the crowd, his eyes fixed on Bruce the way a predator does with its prey. However, as if caught in a fishing net, he forgot about his task and let himself be carried away by Mester's words.

"Juan, your turn has finally come." Mester signaled for the man to join him. "We will enter the Merkaba together, and I will direct it. All you have to do is let yourself be carried."

With nothing to lose, Juan positioned himself inside the Merkaba next to Mester. His heart was beating so fast that he was sure it would give out any second.

Mester softly placed a hand on his shoulder, "Juan just close your eyes and focus on your breathing, this will calm your mind and relax your body for the journey".

Suddenly Juan felt a strong pull to unite with his spirit self, passing through a bright light at the end of a warm tunnel. *'How odd,'* he thought, *'I had never noticed how many shades of blue there are.*' Floating above an endless ocean, he dipped his hands into the water watching the drips form increasing circles, somehow completely taking away his pain with them. All his traces of doubt were gone. *Heaven*, he breathed, *this must be heaven.* His eyes caught a butterfly briefly before he saw three blurry silhouette figures approaching him. They had no distinct facial features, but he did not need his eyes to tell him who they were.

"My dear Juan, it brings me so much joy that you can see how happy we are here. We have been praying for you. Now that you know the truth, I ask that you be happy. We will end up together. Meanwhile, why not enjoy the journey of your life?"

In that moment, he could no longer recall the pain of losing his family, it had been completely washed away. He was wrapped in God's perfect love. He felt whole once again with a strong desire to stay.

"It's time to go, Juan," Mester advised gently.

With the love of his wife and children engraved in his heart, the scene before him reversed, slowly pulling him out.

Hundreds of eyes watched Juan transform his face of agony into one of hope—something they had not seen in him since his family had died. Tears flowed down his face as he opened his eyes, smiling radiantly.

The crowd waited to hear what he had just seen. They yelled out questions. "What happened? Did you see your family? Why are you crying?"

"I saw them, and if I had to describe that place, I would say that no words exist here on Tellus to explain its beauty. The peacefulness is overpowering. Instead of breathing air, you breathe in love from everywhere. I could see my past with them, my present, and my future all at once. Time does not exist, and my family is eternally happy. When you saw me cry, I was not crying for them, I was crying for all the time I have wasted imagining something that was not real. They were the ones who were worried for me in this world of pain. Thank you, Mester! I have no way of repaying you for this beautiful gift. You have given me back my happiness, and with it, a desire to keep living."

"You have nothing to thank me for, Juan. Your intuition brought you to me. You have more faith than you know. Do not underestimate your power of creation, and you will do great things." Between the hugs and smiles, they celebrated the return of Juan's happiness.

6

The Threat of King Aldon

Sivilion, unable to believe what he had just witnessed, immediately and discretely returned to the palace to report it to the king.

"Your Majesty, I must inform you that Bruce's sudden change is due to a person named Mester. He is someone who comes from space and operates a strange spaceship." The duality in Tellus had caused Sivilion to interpret what he had seen incorrectly due to his limited comprehension.

"What? Impossible!" King Aldon raised his eyebrows, with a wicked expression. "Bring him before me immediately!"

It did not take long for Sivilion to return to the river, where the majority of people had left. Only a handful had stayed behind to help Mester and Domino move the Merkaba back to the workshop. They placed it on the carriage and were about to cover it when the sudden sound of hoof beats drew their attention.

"Stop! The king has asked for your immediate presence."

Hazar went pale. The soldiers moved toward Mester to take him by force.

"Wait!" Domino cried out. "Do not lay a hand on Mester! My son and I will willingly follow you."

They took the carriage that held the Merkaba as evidence and, despite pleading and insults from the small crowd around them, the soldiers took the two men.

"Why are you taking them? They've done nothing wrong!" People yelled in anger. Hazar was at a loss. She wanted to believe it was a terrible nightmare from which she would soon wake, but the shouts from the people around her assured her the contrary.

The steady, heavy-spirited drumroll of a soldier's march accompanied Domino and Mester's heartbeat. An hour later, a twelve feet iron gate opened, announcing their arrival at the palace. Splendid gardens lined the walls of the palace, with heavy scent of exotic flowers perfuming the air. An open porch at the front held up with ostentatiously detailed pillars, painted in gold. Inside all floors were marble and the stairs were ornate with mahogany. Hundreds of portraits of King Aldon painted in oil hung in gold frames; it was almost impossible to stop thinking about him every step of the way.

After a long walk, they finally entered the throne room. Sitting on the king's chair was a pair of bloodshot eyes twitching uncomfortably under greased black hair. His face looked like a mask, with no expressions under his calculated glare.

"Who do we have here? You do not look like an alien. They told me you have a spaceship. Is that right?" Domino tried to answer, but the king stopped him. "I asked Mester." King Aldon spoke with a brazen, yet intimidating voice.

"I have no spaceship, sir." Mester spoke calmly.

"Then what do you carry in that carriage?"

"It's a geometric figure that I built with the help of my father."

King Aldon approached the Merkaba only to see wooden sticks. "I see it's a wooden figure." He glared menacingly at Sivilion. "So, why has my employee, Bruce, my right hand, changed so much? What have you done to him? Is it witchery?"

"Sir, I can assure you that I do not practice witchery. I simply look for a way to help those who need it."

"Then tell me what Bruce needed help with given that he has everything he wants. I pay him extremely well."

"I wasn't referring to money, sir. The type of help I gave him is something money can't give."

"You mean to say you can give him a type of help I can't? What type of help is that?"

"Spiritual help."

"Oh, so you see spirits but deny practicing witchery?" King Aldon's face was smug.

"I was referring to the aches of the spirit, sir—the origin of sadness. That's all." Mester was careful not to give too many details before such ignorance, knowing the problems it could bring him.

Try as he might, King Aldon could not find anything wrong in his explanation. "I will let you go, but I do not want to hear about any more crowds surrounding you. You could be creating a plot against me, and I will not allow that. I am the only leader here. Is that clear?"

"Yes, sir," Mester responded.

Domino and Mester left the palace. It was beginning to get dark. With arms tightly wrapped around their bodies, they faced the strong winds stroking their skin along the path. Domino was walking unusually slowly; his eyes were plastered on the floor as if his brain was figuring out a solution with every step he made. Not even the mosquitos that were breeding in the shallow water left after the morning rain could distract him.

Are you okay father? Mester's eyes showed gentle concern.

Domino laid his hand lightly on Mester's shoulder, "As soon as we get home, we will collect our things. We will leave first thing tomorrow morning."

"Leave? To where, Father?"

"I don't know. Any place will be better than here. I cannot rest knowing you are in danger. You are very well known here. How could we keep so many people away from you? It would be impossible." Fear sat heavy on Domino's heart.

"But, Father, why do you think I want to keep all these people away from me?" Mester turned to his father in confusion. "I explained to you that I came to Tellus to show you the correct path. Please don't let your fear blind your heart, Father."

Domino breathed deeply. He felt that allowing Mester to achieve his dream would mean saying goodbye. No longer wishing to continue talking about this matter, he hugged his son tightly. "Let's hurry home. It's late, and I'm sure your mother is worried sick."

Sunk into the couch on the porch was Hazar, the fresh air usually helped clear her thoughts. Every muscle felt tight. The air was thick and somehow the aroma from the coffee in her hands facilitated her breathing. The steam that had risen from the coffee was gone when she saw two men approaching her.

"Oh my God! What did they do to you? Are you all right? Tell me what happened!" Her blinking lashes were heavy with tears.

Mester and Domino looked at each other, neither one wanting to worry her more than necessary. Finally, Domino spoke. "Everything is okay, my love. It was just a misunderstanding on the king's part. They thought the Merkaba was a spaceship."

"That's all?" Hazar kept asking, feeling like there was more to the story.

"Mother, everything is in perfect order. Not everyone understands my purpose here on Tellus, but I know that you and Father will always support me, right?"

"Of course." She smiled while Domino remained silent. "You both must be starving. Sit down while I serve dinner."

They sat deep in silence. The air was different. Everyone was moving, but there was no talking. There was no sound in the house except for the faucet dripping into the sink.

Hazar was sure that something was wrong. Scanning their faces for answers was making her eyes ache, until a knock on the door interrupted.

They were terrified, imagining the worst, but their fear washed away by the sight of Mester's followers.

"We've come to find out how Mester is doing. Is he okay? How may we help?"

Mester approached the door. He could not contain his excitement at the sight of all these people. However, Domino and Hazar did not share his excitement.

"Thank you all for coming. Please come inside."

Domino eyed the crowd and then looked at Hazar, questioning how they will fit so many people in the house. She did not say a word; instead, she showed a big comfortable smile. Deep down she preferred that commotion than the silence that ladled her ears. With open arms she guided them in, helping them feel comfortable, on every chair, rug, and corner.

"The king has asked that I do not call the attention of a crowd. He fears I might challenge his power." Mester began.

"Does this mean that you won't continue to teach us?" The crowd asked with great sorrow.

"No, of course not! I came to Tellus to help you all, and I will. We just have to figure out a way to avoid calling so much attention to ourselves."

Lost in thought, Juan said, "I have heard others talk about an island not far from here called Moorea. It is only accessible every twelve years when the star of Sirio is positioned above the island. During midnight of the full moon when this occurs, a canal opens, revealing an entry and exit to Moorea before it close for another twelve years. Our ancestors claimed that this is how long it took for our conscience to evolve."

A million thoughts crossed Domino's mind.

"But once it's closed, you can exit the island on a boat, I imagine?" Domino questioned.

Juan was pessimistic, "It's been a long time since anyone has tried it. The currents there are so strong that they sweep away anything on its waters. They call it the Dragon Belt."

The idea seemed farfetched to some, but a tiny current moved through Mester's body, and the goosebumps rising on his skin showed him his intuition was right on target. "When does the canal open next?" he asked with great urgency.

"Whether by coincidence or not, it opens tomorrow at midnight during the full moon, for just one hour. After that, the canal will seal the path for the next twelve years."

Hazar and Domino were trying to coordinate their thoughts. What would they do with the workshop? The house? How would they sell it so soon? Everything was happening very quickly.

Deep in thought, Mester studied those present before speaking. The timing of it all made it very clear to Mester "Juan, tomorrow morning, when the sun rises, please direct me to Moorea." He paused, and then whispered, "Those who wish to join me are more than welcome."

The crowd was dead silent. The wood from the fireplace was nearly gone, just as time was running out to make a decision. Seeing that no one said a word, Mester added, "Do not feel pressured. I understand that leaving your homes, families, and jobs is no easy task. The path to a better future is unknown to you and will always be accompanied by high risks. If it were not, you would not appreciate it, and it would lose its appeal. Take the night to think. Tomorrow, as soon as the sun is up, I will meet you at the river and leave from there, with whoever wishes to join me. For now, it may be a good idea for you all to rest."

The door screeched, announcing the last exit. The living room felt empty, emptier than ever before. The dense air added unnecessary weight to their lungs. Domino and Hazar were sitting on the sofa closest to the chimney, holding hands very tightly as if scared to let go. They knew that their son had an adventurous spirit, but this was too much.

Juan remained behind to talk with Mester. "I am in debt to you. I want you to know that I will go with you. I will support you in whatever you may need."

"Let's be reasonable!" Domino suddenly yelled. "Why take such a risk going to a place like that?"

"Father, I will not turn my back on my mission. Moorea will give me the opportunity to share my wisdom without King Aldon's influence. There, my companions will learn astrology and geometry, as well as other necessities for the evolution of Tellus. Here in Tallen, I will not have that time. I must leave a mark so strong that it will last through the history of Tellus. I must make sure that my coming here was not in vain."

"How can I leave my job, my workshop, my clients, and my house? We will not have enough…"

"Then you should both stay. It will be best, especially as my journey will not be easy. This path is not yours to take. It's mine."

"What? That is impossible, Mester. I wouldn't dream of it!" Hazar yelled in such desperation that her tone would have broken anyone's heart.

Mester moved closer with those eyes that could look deeply into hers as he hugged her tightly, comforting her. He could not leave her in this state.

"Please, don't go," she begged him, falling to her knees.

Mester quickly picked her up with tenderness. "My beloved Mother, love is not about possession, but about appreciation. Would you rather have me here as one of King Aldon's slaves or even dead? Or would you want me far away and happy as I complete my mission?"

These words came together as if they were the pieces of a puzzle in Hazar's heart. She imagined her son ripped away from his freedom, stuck in a dark dungeon, destined to spend the rest of his life there. Color returned to her cheeks, and her expression changed as she turned to her son, with strength now replacing her desperation.

"You're right, Mester. I want you to be free and happy. I just ask that you let me be there for you when you depart on your journey."

Her words surprised Domino so much that he preferred to remain quiet so as not to ruin this tender moment between mother and son.

7

The Journey to Moorea

A majestic sunrise awoke, red orange glow seeping over the horizon. Powerful rays flooded over the landscape, lighting every blade of grass. The river shone as if diamonds were running through its waters, while hummingbirds fluttered their wings frantically, changing colors in the sunlight.

Yes! Today will be a grand day! Mester thought as he was walking to the river accompanied by his parents. All he had taken with him was an old leather backpack that Domino used for his trips. Hazar had filled it with everything she could, using the magic all mothers use to pack for their children.

The lake mirrored the sky above, in addition to Juan's body who got there early to take a bath. The water was uncommonly clear, so much that it was impossible to not see every playful turn Juan made.

"Look, there is Juan," Hazar pointed out.

"Juan has such a free spirit, one that is a treasure to have close by." Mester smiled.

As they watched Juan taking a bath, soft footsteps echoed behind them, trampling the leaves on the grass. A small group of people drew near, with their luggage in tow, giving the impression that they were all ready to go.

The Creator of the Universe

Child-like excitement filled Mester from head to toe. Among the travelers were six women. He had not expected such a feminine presence for such a risky journey. It took a second or two for him to realize that Lucia was among them. He would have never imagined that her mother would allow her to go after having almost lost her.

"Lucia, does your Mom know about this?" Hazar asked.

"Yes, Mrs., she told me that just knowing I am alive and am accompanying Mester brings more than enough comfort to her. She preferred to say good bye at home," Lucia replied, eyes watering.

The other five women introduced themselves.

"Hi Mester, my name is Cayenna."

"Mine Elissa."

"I am Alline."

"Isabel."

"And since they saved the best for last, I am Eloisa." She said with a sly wink.

They were disarmingly beautiful. Something radiated from them that rendered them irresistible to the opposite gender, apart from their meager clothing.

"We are women of the streets, but after we heard you talk, Mester, our lives changed. We felt relieved by your messages, but it was a relief that left us hungry for more. We do not want small sips; we want to find the source of the spring."

These words stunned everyone. In three days, Mester had achieved something amazing. Hope was drawn to each person who listened to Mester's words. Deep down they all wondered what he would be capable of in twelve years.

Minutes later, a group of four men approached, "Good morning Mester! If it is all right with you, we are ready to accompany you. My name is Eriiiseooo." His yawns were contagious among the rest, with all his shirt-buttons done up in the wrong holes.

"I am Eloin."

"My name is Thomas."

Last, came a very tall man. He had a pencil-mustache. His nose was impossibly straight, barely able to sustain his big, squared magnified glasses, making his eyes look like he was standing too close. He carried with him a jacket with pockets so packed that it rather looked like a backpack instead. He was no doubt ready for the journey.

"I am Dr. Geo. People call me that because I know so much about Tellus' geography that I may as well have created it."

Mester could not help but remember YinYang. *With one, we have enough.*

Strangely, a black butterfly settled gently on Mester's shoulders, and then flew in circles around him, as if trying to tell him something.

I cannot thank you all enough for coming with me. It will not be an easy journey, but one we will always remember. I think it's time we depart," Mester insisted.

"Mother, Father, I think it's best we say goodbye here. The terrain is not easy, and you will face greater risk traveling at night."

Hazar's eyes were filled with tears. Mester hugged her once more and a minute went by in silence, as their bodies said everything they could not say to each other. He wiped the tears from his mother's face. "From now on, if you are to cry over me, let it be from happiness at the thought that your son is completing his mission."

Once again, Mester had managed to give her the extra strength she needed. "I will do just that, my son. Even though you will not be able to see me from there, I will be smiling for you."

Domino squeezed his son's hand and pulled him into a hug. He wanted to cry, but after hearing what he'd just told Hazar, he refrained. "I am very proud of you. I know you will go above and beyond, just as you have always done. May love always guide and protect you."

With these words nourishing his soul, Mester turned to the rest to start the journey. Even though he would not show it, his heart was broken, but his mission had to prevail for the good of all Telluranians.

"Please let me guide you," Dr. Geo took the chance to take control. "See that mountain? Well, that is Alekos, and behind it is Moorea. We must climb to the top to descend from behind. It will not be an easy journey." His eyebrows rose with a fixed look at the group.

Alekos was a gigantic red barrier, marked by sharp peaks, rising like an enormous wall without interruption at seven thousand feet of elevation above the tender undulations of the prairie.

Several faces showed the adequate level of insecurity at the thought of having to cross the mountain before them, especially Eloin, who was huge in every way, tall with a belly as wide as the length of his leg.

"Do not worry, it looks worse than what it actually is," Dr. Geo replied, but his comments were not very encouraging.

They began the journey. Soon, a narrow valley marked the beginning of an adventure. A journey of about ten kilometers lay before them until they could reach the base of the mountain. Forests replaced the cultivated fields and the beautiful rocky mountains framed the scenario with beautiful springs adding a melody to the land.

Curiously, every time they sat down to rest, despite having more than enough time before midnight, several signs appeared before Mester, reminding him that time was critical.

The Creator of the Universe

First, a huge animal leaped from the river, crawling behind them with great evil and had skin of stones giving it an invincible appearance. Following this, a mockingbird sat on a nearby tree branch, singing a fast melody and moving its head from side to side as if it was clockwork, trying to speed them along. Finally, the road twisted, winding around old trees, with branches so wide, making it the ideal place to take a break and rest. Without any detectable noise, a black mamba snake, eight feet in length, approached Mester and raised his head with an open mouth ready to devour him. One bite was enough poison to kill all dozen of them.

"Don't you dare!" Juan took a stick beside him and without hesitating, hit his head. The animal tumbled, giving them barely enough time to escape. Mester did not know exactly what was happening, but he now understood they had to pick up the pace.

They continued by following a footpath through the woods. The path rose in steepness, with uneven rocky steps. Each footstep cost them more of their strength.

"Are we there yet?" asked Cayenna, panting. She had the hair pulled into a ponytail, and her lips that were once pink and soft, were now chapped. She looked tired.

"Almost," Mester placed a firm arm on her shoulder.

After a ten-hour hike, they reached the peak of the mountain. An exclamation of release escaped from their mouths... "Ah-mazing!" With a three hundred and sixty degree, a breathtaking view opened before them. All of Tallen could be seen from there.

"Look!" yelled Juan with joy. "There's Moorea!"

Their eyes settled on it for a moment. "Beautiful!" A collection of waterfalls of about eighty feet formed the frontier of the beautiful island in the shape of a heart. Strangely enough, as the water neared the waterfalls, the color of the water changed from its typical bluish color to one with a tint of red in it. At the center of the island, one large mountain took center stage, mostly covered in greenery except for its snowy peaks.

"What could that island possibly hold? How strange…I have never in my life seen anything like this, and look at that red color…" Juan was spinning with questions.

"That red color marks the Belt of the Dragon," affirmed Dr. Geo.

"This is impossible. There must be a mistake." Lucia turned to Mester. "How do you suppose we get down there? It seems to me like a suicide mission… I am not the world's best swimmer, but even if I were, I would need to be something more than a fish to get down there."

Among the panic, Lucia's comment brought about several laughs.

"Do you really believe I would allow for anything to happen to you?" Mester looked at her with tender of eyes.

"No, of course not."

"So then, have faith. Remember that our paths lie before us. We just have to co-create them. Right now, there is no set path, but that doesn't mean we won't find it." With one wink, Mester brought out the courage Lucia needed.

Mester wondered, *what could possibly be so special about this island for nature to guard its entry so cautiously, and for so many years?* "Let's not waste any time. We must arrive as soon as possible."

Juan frowned in confusion. "But we still have until midnight. What is the hurry?"

"I don't know Juan, but we have had enough signs to rush along our journey. Let's trust in them."

They walked to the closer cliff, with its sheer curtains of solid rock holding them up to the sky.

Eloin sigh in a deep breath, he was on the verge of hysterics after looking down the cliff. "I have had a fear of heights for as long as I can remember." His tracksuit was so wet that it revealed the rolls around his belly with his hair plastered to his scalp. "What will we do? We do not have the necessary tools to hike down into this abyss." He was well aware of his own physical limitations, but this went far beyond having any physical ability, climbing down the cliff would be the end for them all.

"Look over there! There is a massive crack in the middle of the mountain. Let's take a closer look!" There were few things that Dr. Geo loved more than an adventure.

Cautiously, they moved closer, and extending their necks beyond their given length, they managed to take a closer look into the interior. This fracture appeared to connect them to the bottom of the mountain, intersected by some window openings toward the ocean. Curiously, at the center, hundreds of trunks intertwined, forming bridges from one side to the other.

Mester took the lead. "Juan and Thomas, please help me down, I want to try something." He climbed onto one of the trunks. From there, he could see that all the branches connected across this gap with no inclination. Using these to descend was not a viable option.

The barks were so smooth that they felt more like skin. "I could touch these branches all day. What a pleasant sensation they give," Mester felt something different.

When the trunk felt contact with Mester it rose like a horse reeling from joy. For a full half-minute, he went up and down at a speed that constricted his throat, making it nearly impossible to breathe. He felt his body move in ways it should not. Just before falling, he managed to cling onto an unexpected growing vine. Slowly, the trunk began to calm down until it placed itself in a slight inclination, just enough to allow him to descend onto the next level.

Recuperating from the fright, Mester wiped the sweat from his forehead with the sleeve of his shirt. "Well then, I believe it is now safe for you all to go down, but please be careful."

The Creator of the Universe

Holding each other hand in hand, they followed Mester. They moved down onto the second branch and eventually each trunk got easier and easier. As they moved down, the trunks silently kept growing more vines, forming a green leaved curtain. The light from the moon that slipped through the window openings faded until the view of the ocean was completely blocked by the vines. The place became as dark as the mouth of a wolf. The temperature rose incredibly fast and the humidity made the trunks even more slippery.

"I can't see anything, help meeeee...!" Juan slipped and fell. His screams now grew further away.

Mester felt every ounce of skin on his body cringe; he assumed the worst, along with the rest.

Juan found himself falling in the darkness, hurtling towards an invisible floor. Caught in a superman pose he felt himself suspended in the air. Something kept turning around his waist as he began to rise instead of fall. *Am I dreaming...? Or maybe dead?*

In between maneuvers, Dr. Geo grabbed a shirt from his bag, and wrapped it around the stick he had in his hand and said, "Whether navigating the woods or hunting for treasure, who doesn't grab a dry wooden stick along a journey in case you need a torch." Confidently, he took a box of matches from one of his pockets, shook it for far too long as if adding a little more to his ego, and set the cloth on fire. He moved the torch in search of faces and as he turned around there stood Juan.

"Juan what happened? We thought you had fallen?"

"I thought I had too. I mean I felt as if I had but something brought me back," said Juan as he shook off the roots stuck to his shirt.

"Mmmm..." Dr. Geo looked back at him with his eyebrows raised, but did not answer as he was lost in thought about the possible decline of Juan's mental sanity. In that moment, the intertwined vines fell before his face as it bloomed a flower in the shape of a monkey's face for a span of three seconds.

"Did you guys see that?"

"What?"

"Nothing... nevermind." He thought it was best to keep this to himself.

With the torch, the crooked shadows came, "Uuuuuhhhh" yelled Thomas attempting to scare them when suddenly another vine opened a flower before his eyes. This time, it had the shape of a skull. Thomas' scream was so loud it seemed to echo within their heads.

"What happened, Thomas?" Yelled Dr. Geo in anger from the headache he felt coming on.

"I don't know, but I do know that one of you is playing a prank on me. I urge you to stop because this is no time for games."

A flower in the shape of a peaceful dove now appeared before everyone and in a sweet voice, it said:

"There was once a tiger; beautiful, able and strong
He carried himself with elegance, sure of his supremacy
He hunted upon whichever animal he pleased
One day came a man who pointed at him with a gun
The tiger retreated his ego and begged for compassion."

There was not a single reaction, not even one from Mester.

"Don't tell me you've never seen a flower speak? I am not the only one either; let me present you to my fellow mates." The curtain of vines rose as hundreds of flowers appeared before them. There were infinite amounts of different faces waiting to greet them. "We are the Cliffhangers and through our stories and riddles we help consciousness grow. We only grow when Moorea is about to open, surviving for only a few hours after the Dragon Belt closes. After which, one by one, we fall to the ground, giving way for the next cycle of life. As you understand, our time is very limited so, go on! They're waiting for their applause," said the flower with the face of a peaceful dove.

Still lost in confusion, they followed the instructions. They moved their hands, lacking rhythm.

"Thank you, thank you. Very well, now that we have presented ourselves, it is now your turn."

"Ehh... Pardon me," Mester responded by introducing his friends and then added, "We came to enter Moorea, but where are we?"

"This is the mother rock, Alekos. We tell her stories through the hundreds of characters that we have. Her wisdom preserves the safety of this place, and even more so Moorea. She will welcome you and she wishes to speak with you all."

They stood in silence waiting to hear a new voice.

In that moment, the face of a little clown appeared, "How about you touch the walls of this rock and see if you can hear her," it said in a very ironic tone. This voice laughed incessantly as if they had just said the funniest of jokes.

Dr. Geo was beginning to feel uncomfortable.

Lucia was the first one. She turned around and put her hands among the rocks. "What is this place?" As a response, when she lowered her hand, the surface began to move with subtle movements. It looked like a caterpillar covered in precious stones, almost like a moving amethyst. With every movement, the crystals reflected light, finally illuminating the area as she heard voices that told stories.

"Why did the rock not light up for me?" Dr. Geo asked while he fixed his glasses, hiding his confusion.

The small face of a peaceful dove said in a tender voice:

> "To know, you must see
> To be wise, close your eyes
> So you will know
> What has been in your heart all along."

Dr. Geo closed his eyes with suspicion and silenced himself for a few seconds. The expression on his face lit up, "Yes, I hear it!" He could not hide his excitement, for this was a great accomplishment for him.

These stories touched them on a very profound level, awakening their long dormant consciences as well as their connection with the space around them. They continued in silence to support the mother rock in a conscious manner, knowing that everything they touched was alive.

If they for one second thought that their descent would be boring, well the Cliffhangers made sure to change their mind. When it came to extraordinary hiking skills, the intertwined vines took first place. They were restless and overjoyed to have them as company. This was a rare experience for them; finally had spectators after twelve years. Moving freely in entertaining ways, they narrated their popular stories.

> "A great rainbow of a sun lying down awaits you
> Its center shall sustain you
> Up until the epitomes come
> For the creation to be done."

This story rumbled like a storm deep inside of Mester, as he hummed a tune trying to memorize it.

The vines were extremely intelligent, as well as sensitive. They had already perceived the connection that lay between Mester and Lucia, which is why they waited until just before reaching the very bottom to give them a surprise.

The Creator of the Universe

Between all the jumping and raucous Lucia felt a firm grip around her waist. For a moment, she thought it was Mester, and she looked straight at him, but he appeared to have nothing to do with it. *Hmm... it could not be Mester. He would never initiate anything with how timid he is.*

"Hahahaha"....She could hear the vines laughing.

"Of course! The Cliffhangers must be behind it," Lucia thought.

In that moment the vines now gripped Mester, and with eyes full of surprise, he turned to Lucia. Before they could ask one another what was happening the vines intertwined them in a spiral manner until they were face to face, placing their bodies closer than they had ever been. Their cheeks flushed as the Cliffhangers told a story of love.

"Two hearts shone in the sky
They were contemplating without rest
The distance seemed an impediment
To shine in a single light."

For a moment, Mester let himself be carried away by his emotions. Unexpectedly, however, Losna's features began taking life in Lucia's face. The Cliffhangers perceived this and immediately let them go.

"Look, we have arrived!" Yelled Juan.

The vines had served as such a great distraction that they had lost track of time. Moorea was now only two miles away. They walked to shore, feeling a sense of relief as they soaked their aching, scratched feet.

"How will we possibly get there?" Elissa thought aloud.

The same way we came down the mountain, Mester looked at her mischievously.

"With the vines?" Dr. Geo did not want anything more to do with them.

"I was referring to the way that we co-created the path to arrive here," Mester responded.

The moonlight shone on the water like a pale silver path, lessening the blackness of the night. At a distance, in the hills, lay a line of silhouettes against the velvety sky. With an impressive display of horses, each soldier carried with them a flaming red flag with the face of a skull printed upon them, leaving no doubt in their minds, it was King Aldon's cavalry. They looked like gruesome beasts in full armor waiting for the hunt.

That morning, Sivilion had found out about Mester's intentions to head to Moorea and quickly informed the king. Anger boiled deep in King Aldon's blood. The king had almost gone mad at the thought of losing track of Mester, realizing how dangerous that could be for him. Mester had become his worst nightmare from the first day he met him. It was as if his intuition warned him that he was no ordinary man. He immediately ordered for every pathway to Moorea to be blocked off.

Two hours had passed since Sivilion had arrived at the peak of Alekos. For those two hours, he did not dare blink his eyes as he stood guard. The tenseness in his muscles made him look like a stone figure.

"My captain, look over there! There are people down there! But how did they manage to get all the way there without us noticing?" Asked Natzuel, second in command, with his nose and forehead scrunched up.

Sivilion focused his binoculars among the group. At just the sight of Mester, a sudden gush of pain jolted throughout Sivilion's body. Fires of fury were smoldering in his small narrowed eyes. His attempts to detain him before going downhill had clearly failed, but he did not intend to look like a fool as a master of war. The trumpets of war went off and with his blade pointing forward; He ordered the cavalry to descend at full speed. If Mester flees, he will lose his place as captain, or maybe even his own life.

8

The Intervention of the Gods

The gods were watching everything that occurred on Tellus, and had not for an instant take their attention off Brahman. While their other creations continued along the natural course of their evolutions, the gods focused on YinYang's creation, like a mother focused on helping her most helpless child.

Looking upon the king's guards surrounding the group of travelers reminded the Creator of the pain he felt when Brahman left him. There was still too much time before the force of the moon would open their path to Moorea. What would they do to get out of this predicament? A million scenarios and questions crossed the Creator's mind.

"Mester doesn't appear to have it easy." YinYang's eyes lit up, and his lips curved in malicious pleasure. He felt he had an ally in King Aldon.

The gods shared a great resentment toward YinYang. With each passing day, the Creator's hopes for his odd creation diminished. He had not seen one positive change in YinYang, and he did not seem to care about the obstacles Brahman was facing because of him.

Losna missed her friend, but it was only now that she saw Mester next to Lucia that she realized how much he meant to her.

The Creator of the Universe

Losna's eyes were frozen over Tellus. Brahman was at a crossroads. Her power grew stronger than it had ever been and with it, her ability to intervene. She had to do something, or she would lose him.

"Wait, you cannot alter the cycle on Tellus," YinYang interrupted, as if giving an order. "That goes against the rules."

For the first time, the gods confronted one another. "What rules, YinYang? On Tellus, there are no fair rules. All you've created is a mess!" How is it you see this suffering and choose to do nothing? Losna finally said what everyone else had been thinking.

There was silence. The Creator did not dare blink even one of his eyes.

"I have authorization to intervene because the original rules state that we can do so to help one another—not that you'd understand that concept," Losna sneered. Without wasting any more time, she directed her stare to Tellus' moon:

> "Beautiful moon with the magic you bring
> Accelerate the speed of your swing,
> Reveal now the path to Moorea for one hour,
> Before hiding your great power."

YinYang's swelling veins were waiting to explode. Once again, the others had gotten their way. He could not disguise it. The scale above his head was left fully leaning towards his dark side, showing anything but balance.

9

The Dragon Belt

The flags of the soldiers were waving, signaling the danger that was to come. There were still two hours left until midnight, enough time for the troops to descend. As the wind danced in between the vines, fear flooded their conscience accompanied by the furious soundtrack of the horses above them.

Mester refused to believe this was the way it all ended after everything they had gone through to get here. His gazed switched between the king's men and Moorea.

The struggle taking place in his thoughts disappeared, replaced with the sensation of having been dropped into a mixer.

"Earrrrthquaaaake!" yelled Dr. Geo.

At first no one moved, their brains were unable to make sense of the input from their senses. The earth began to move as if it was a huge wave, and the intensity with which the sand convulsed made it feel like it was piercing into their bodies

"Oh myyy Godddd! What is happening?" shouted Cayenna, jiggling as the water beneath her feet flowed away completely from shore.

"Look! The waters are stirring!" yelled Juan. "But it's still not midnight..."

"It is actually ten pm," Dr. Geo clarified.

The Creator of the Universe

A new looming on the horizon appeared. Losna's power of magnetism had caused the moon to accelerate its cycles. The level of the water kept depleting until an extensive rug of sand appeared beneath their feet, revealing a pathway to Moorea.

Many sea creatures faded away with the ocean, while several others took temporary refuge in the small puddles left behind. The smallest of them hidden in between rocky cracks while others attempted to survive among the humidity of the intertwined algae.

"Who would have guessed? Arriving to Moorea by foot definitely was not in my plans," Lucia said with a sigh of relief.

Mester was not the least bit surprised. This very fortunate turn of events had Losna written all over it. The air of the night had never tasted so sweet. He imagined her long white hair covering her mysterious features, wishing more than anything to have her standing before him. The moon's glow pierced his gaze so intensely that he felt it reach his soul.

"Hurry!" screamed Elissa. "The soldiers are descending the mountains, we have to run!" Her cry brought Mester back to the moment.

The earthquake caused the soldiers' horses to act out in fear. With wild roars, they threw every single soldier to the ground fleeing in terror, leaving the soldiers to the mercy of the night.

When the earthquake finally stopped, Sivilion stood up slightly stunned as he attempted to regain his balance. "Very well. We will continue by foot!"

The vines danced from side to side. They were as happy as could be as they anxiously awaited their next guests. When vines sensed their intentions, they left them to fend for themselves. The soldiers began to descend without any help, consumed by complete darkness. They tried to

The Creator of the Universe

support themselves with the vines as they playfully twisted their wrists and ankles in hopes of slowing down their pace. In between stumbles, their trip down the mountain turned into a nightmare. The only thing the Cliffhangers did not like was not being able to share their stories, having to keep quiet was a punishment for them.

Mester and the rest sped up their pace toward Moorea. Dr. Geo searched for the flattest landscape to cut down time while using his hat to scare away the seagulls eyeing the small fish for a potential buffet.

At just one hundred feet from the Dragon Belt, Elissa entered into panic, "Look! What is that jumping over there?"

"Sharks," Dr. Geo responded nonchalantly. "I must say, I have never seen so many of them, especially ones so big..."

Like flying fish, sharks with crushing pavement teeth were jumping with grate force. Though it may have looked like a coordinated attack by an underwater army, it was actually an escape mechanism in an attempt to accommodate themselves within the small available puddles.

A forest made of red coral, rising to an impressive height of thirty feet, formed the edges of the island. The coral reef had a gorgeous mass of flowers called The Red Snare. Its color was a deep red, almost like blood, which ironically was the shark's favorite meal. Within the flower was a hidden mouth with small tentacles capable of trapping and digesting small animals. This, alongside their revolting smell, kept all living things away from them, except the sharks. The currents of the waterfall carried with it their potent odor, attracting enough sharks to guard the island.

"Do not worry. Follow me and watch out for the coral. Their beauty makes it difficult to abstain from reaching out a hand to touch them. This specific species can be toxic to touch, potentially even deadly because of their Red Snare

Flowers, and they're carnivorous." Dr. Geo loved to give long explanations and enjoyed the look of shock that crept upon their faces, even though more often than not, he pushed his comments too far.

"Dr. Geo you speak as if the only problem is the coral and the Red Snare Flowers, but what about the sharks?" Elissa asked as she raised her eyebrows, trying to make sense of it all.

"Ah, do not worry about those for now, just think of them as jumping frogs, so let's hurry it up."

"Jumping frogs...." Elissa was not the least bit amused by this.

Despite this, they moved in a single file line, following every one of Dr. Geo's footsteps. Somehow, the confidence with which he walked brought them a sense of safety. As they moved along, the coral became much denser and the level of difficulty to maneuver around them grew greater.

The suffocating odor did not help, causing the group to feel nauseous. It was overwhelmingly intense, as if they were walking inside an actual dumpster.

"I can't walk anymore. I feel like I may pass out," Lucia bent over, gagged and vomited between her legs.

Mester caught her as her legs began to give out and pulled out his handkerchief, "Cover your nose with this. It'll help with the smell."

Lucia gradually began to recover. Mester's smell on the handkerchief was just the remedy she needed.

"How odd? How can such a beautiful flower give off such a horrendous smell?" Isabel complained, not realizing she was getting too close to one of them.

"Help! Help me! Noo!" Isabel cried out. The sticky flower trapped her skirt, pulling her to its beak, only seconds away from being devoured.

"I knew that at some point I would have to use it," Dr. Geo opened his backpack and pulled out a giant butcher's knife, it had a dual blade with a hardwood handle. "Isn't it a beauty? With just one move, he managed to slit the base of the flower, liberating a bloodlike liquid that splashed all over them. It was like blood gushing in a constant flow, whose smell altered the sharks, making their jumps grow with anger.

Dr. Geo took the flower and quickly launched it to the sharks to calm them down, even if it was just for a moment. "We still have a long way to go, so I suggest that you pay attention and don't touch anything." He raised his tone, aiming his gaze specifically at Isabel.

After a few steps forward, it was now Elissa crying out in desperation, "My dress! I am stuck! I can't free myself from it!" A giant oyster snapped shut on Elissa's dress.

"Take my hand," yelled Thomas. With one pull, he freed her from the trap, leaving half the dress behind her. "Get on my back. It will be safer." Thomas fixed his hair with one hand, drawing attention to his very muscular frame. He was a living work of art, at least to Elissa that was.

Elissa was shorter than the average woman and had silky blonde hair. She was highly practiced at seduction, but now standing before Thomas it was as if he were the first man to ever stand before her. Thomas leaned down while reaching out to her with one hand. After some hesitation, she accepted his invitation. Her arms around Thomas's neck gave her something more than just a feeling of safety.

The connection within the group kept growing, and due to the high demand of physical intensity, they teamed off in pairs to protect the women. Obviously, Lucia followed Mester's lead, Thomas carried Elissa, Dr. Geo kept an eye on Isabel (he did not want any more surprises), Eriseo gently carried Cayenna by the hand, Juan was with Eloisa, and Eloin watched his backpack of food along with Alline.

Their bodies acted as puppets, they bent in all different directions reaching almost impossible postures in order to avoid touching the coral. They were unbelievably exhausted. The temperature continued to increase and the sweat droplets on their skin flowed endlessly down their faces and limbs.

Dr. Geo was like a magician, from one of the many pockets of his backpack, he pulled out several pieces of cloth. "Here you go. Put this around your forehead if you wish to see where you're walking, unless you want salty beads running into your eyes." The group was no longer amused in the slightest by his jokes.

"I think it's a little late for that," responded Juan, "Look! Moorea!" The island was as radiant as the sun.

"Am I imagining things or is it day there? I think I see light…?" Dr. Geo eyebrows frowned. He looked at his watch with shock written all over his face. "According to my watch, it is eleven o'clock at night." He shook his watch several times to make sure it was working properly.

The rest were only concerned with reaching the island safely. They had reached the edge of the waterfall and now about an eighty-foot drop awaited them. The walls of the waterfall were made of algae net, spongy enough to allow for a firm grip.

"How I wish for the Cliffhangers to be here right now," Eloin whispered aloud. For him it was no simple task to carry his own weight, not to mention the extra weight he carried on his backpack, but he preferred that to leaving his fuel behind.

The laughter did not stop, and Alline sweetly tried to raise his spirits. "Let's go Eloin. You can do this. Soon enough you will be able to eat whatever you like." Those seemed to be the magic words because he was the first one to reach the ground.

If they thought there was an abundant amount of sharks behind them, inside Moorea was the nest. They carefully maneuvered their way around to descend right onto a small hill that served as a bridge to reach the island.

Gradually, the ground below their feet changed from a red color to a fine white sand. They looked around them, taking in every detail. The mountain shimmered with light and everything seemed at peace.

"Mester, what will we do now? The canal opened before it should, and if it does not close until midnight then that will be the end of us," Elissa was barely able to get her words out.

"Have faith Elissa! If the canal opened before time to help us, the same force will do something about it." Mester's assurance was unwavering. There was not a doubt in his mind that Losna had everything under control.

The soldiers had already reached the edge of the waterfalls, there were too many to count. They jumped in desperation driven by the rush of adrenaline given by Sivilion. Their torn suits revealed deep cuts and the odor of blood seemed to antagonize the ferocious animals that waited for them mercilessly.

Suddenly, the same earthquake they had felt a few hours ago returned, but this time with greater intensity. The level of the ocean began to rise and the waterfalls were regaining their strength. From below, they could see how the soldiers attempted to climb the coral in order to avoid the sharks. The great coral forest began losing height and within seconds, the waterfalls took over the scene, dragging everything in their path. The red color that characterized the water intensified into an almost purple color as the hundreds of men disappeared below it.

"No, what horror!" Lucia whimpered, covering her eyes. She could not see such a cruel end to these men. Her nobility was not capable of witnessing such a bloody event.

Mester hugged her trying to provide comfort "I understand how you feel. It's very sad to see how such evil is returned of equal or greater intensity."

No one took any comfort in the events they had just witnessed, but Dr. Geo could not refrain from voicing his feelings. "Well, it came down to either them being dinner for the sharks or us being dinner for King Aldon."

10

The Secret of Moorea

The water around the island was as clear as glass, giving the appearance that the infinite depths of the sea were just a blink away. Multiple sharks swam close to the shoreline, making difficult to forget about their new company.

The island itself was like a fairy-tale garden with an ocean of flowers and exotic trees. The sight was so marvelous and relaxing that all worries would feel like a feint dream.

From a distance, the beautiful waterfalls crashed onto several rocks, giving the effect of many waterfalls rather than just one. The noise had increased steadily and they could no longer shout to one another over the deafening roar of the water.

"I could spend years watching these cascades of water and still never grow tired of such excruciating beauty." Eloisa shouted.

"How does twelve years sound? I just hope that as we move further away from the shore, this stops. I can't imagine twelve years under this mist," Dr. Geo spoke aloud as he tried to rub away the fog from his glasses.

Quite opposite from where they stood, a few feet away from the shore, a pathway of grass stretched out in the direction of the mountain. Looking for any kind of dry refuge, this path appeared to be the best option.

The mountain was vivid green, and at eighty feet in height, the peak was mostly coated in snow. The vegetation was lush, with no trace of civilization in this wild place. Strangely, they noticed that the soil was transparent and the bark of the trees was completely translucent, revealing the plants' secret of life. They could see the water entering through the roots, and the dissolving mineral nutrients traveling upward through the inner barks and into the leaves.

"They look like glass-trees. How is this possible?" Dr. Geo scanned the ground for a sample. "This is too much! Transparent trees. It's daytime at midnight." He took a deep breath to hide his sense of helplessness. It was as if he had lost control since he could not back up his usual rants with facts.

"Does this mean we'll have to sleep during the day?" Eriseo was the kind of person that needed a good night's sleep. He sat, tired-eyed, unshaven and unwashed.

For the rest, that was the least of their concerns.

"How will we feed ourselves? There is no fruit, vegetables or anything that seems the least bit edible." Eloin asked with clear anxiety in his voice. His large belly was not due to genetics, making his good taste for food noticeable. He wore khaki trousers, which must have used enough material to make a tent. He was bald with a brown mustache and had several chins cascading down his neck.

There was much uncertainty; nothing made any logical sense to anyone, except for Mester, "Imagine for one moment that none of you had lived in Tallen. Reprogram your minds and forget about everything you think you know. This is the only way we will be able to notice the signals that will guide us. Let's go on and continue climbing the mountain, I am sure we will find a good place to rest."

As they moved up the mountain, the temperature began to drop dramatically and despite being less than eighty feet above the ground, it was freezing.

Every time, I understand less and less. I have spent my entire life studying the geometry of Tellus and this small island pretends to refute all my knowledge. Cold at eighty feet high? Oh please! Dr. Geo murmured as he walked, hitting the rocks in his way.

A little before reaching the top, they saw trees of great height. Even with their arms fully out-stretched, they would never be able to match even a fraction of the radius of the trunk. The canopy above them looked like clouds of green. This was a perfect place for shelter, allowing them to catch their breath and collect their thoughts.

Only Dr. Geo continued to inspect, while the others settled and opened their bags to unpack. Mester draped his backpack over his legs. The leather was old and stretched, as if it might tear at any second. When he opened it, the contents exploded like a spring of memories. There was the blanket his mother had knitted him when he had turned seven, and despite the distance, he felt his parents' presence now more than ever before. Juan observed Mester removing the contents of his bag—blankets, pillows, changes of clothes, a toothbrush, shoes, his favorite drink (Angel Honey), cookies—but what caught his attention was that there was two of everything.

The Creator of the Universe

"Apparently this isn't only for me," Mester said with a sly smile.

With no shame, Juan crouched onto the opposite side of Mester. Hazar had done the impossible and packed for two, knowing all too well that her son would share what he had.

Lucia opened her small backpack, took out a blanket big enough for all of them to fit, and settled herself. She took out some cookies with a fine layer of chocolate, the same ones her mom used to pack her every morning for school. Of course, these cookies were all too familiar to Mester, since Lucia never failed to share them with him. One by one, she went around offering everyone a cookie.

Eloin accepted the cookie with a puzzled look on his face. *We do not have any food on this island and this girl shares her food as if she had more than enough to last...*

The sound of the waterfall and the pleasant winds were like a lullaby to their ears. They settled down until exhaustion took over. Even the lumpy ground with twisted roots served as a cradle to their tired buddies. Of course, Eriseo was the first one to fall asleep. Before his head reached the ground, his eyes softly closed with a piece of bread still in his mouth.

Surrendered to the breeze, the trees sheltered them. Serenity was plastered across their faces while they slept, except for Mester who looked uncomfortable in any position, rolling from one side to the other. Suddenly he opened his eyes and to his surprise, hundreds of silver-colored mushrooms were staring unblinkingly at him. Each of them had one large eye and was about five inches tall.

What is that? Mester blinked, closed his eyes, and blinked again. *What do they want?* He slowly got up and took a few steps, pausing ever so slightly as the mushrooms aligned themselves, creating a path. Mester understood this sign perfectly and followed them.

The path took him to the very top of the mountain. It was cloudy, and a vast blanket of white hung heavy over the hill. Moving his hands like a fan through the fog, Mester managed to spot several layers of colorful circles on the floor, similar to the pattern of a rainbow. He was hesitant, but in the middle of the silence, a sudden scream frightened the mushrooms.

"Mester! Did you see what I just saw, those eyes...?" Juan was trembling, gasping for air.

The mushrooms were extremely sensitive to fast movements. They correlated velocity with aggression.

"Yes, Juan. They brought me here." Mester put his hand on his shoulder to try to calm him down. "I don't know what this is, but let's go to sleep. We will have enough time tomorrow to figure it out."

Apparently, they were the only ones who had discovered this mysterious phenomenon, everyone else was wrapped in a profound sleep. The only noise could be heard was the ever-present hunger in Eloin; his stomach was growling noisily. They glanced at the clock. It was only three am. Silently, they rejoined the group. Before falling sleep, Mester's thoughts became intertwined with the gods, and the Creator's face became more vivid. He felt comfort in his dreams.

The following day, Juan was the first one up, he was used to waking up in the outdoors, while the rest tossed and turned, trying to organize their things—or more importantly, their thoughts.

Dr. Geo was still lost in sleep. He had his back curved, and the limbs bent and drawn up to his torso. Watching this large man in that position was contrary to his ego.

"Should we wake the captain first?" Juan's wry comment made the group die of laughter.

"What time is it?" Dr. Geo's dream ended abruptly by the noise.

The Creator of the Universe

"Daytime," responded Juan, he did not want to make him feel bad.

"Daytime... It has been daytime since we arrived here," Dr. Geo murmured while folding his blanket.

Mester could not stop thinking about the previous night's event, and wondered if it had been a dream. Suddenly, a spark went off in his head, "Of course, it was the Great Rainbow Sun that the Cliffhangers were talking about."

"What?" Lucia was extremely perceptive and Mester's comment had left her dumbfounded. She was simply going to let it slide when a butterfly took rest upon her shoulder. It was white with silver strips and when it joined its wings, it formed the image of a smile. No one understood why Lucia was hysterically laughing. For a moment, she had forgotten about Mester's odd comment, until the butterfly then took flight into Mester and Juan's direction. *Hmm...well that is strange.*

When Mester and Juan reached the hill, the fog had already dissipated and there was now a colorful disk of ice spinning atop the water.

"How odd?" Mester said, watching the slow rotations and listening to the murmurs of the ice.

They cautiously walked over the surface in search of a sign, but everything seemed normal.

From all the spinning, Juan felt a little sick. "Sorry Mester, I am going to get out of here for a moment. I feel nauseous.

Mester found this strange. Juan was the most energetic person he knew; he never thought that some minor spinning could affect him. Unexpectedly, a familiar voice interrupted them.

"What is that? A spaceship? What does it do?" Lucia jumped onto the surface as she twirled around. "All my life I have dreamed of dancing and now I have the privilege of doing so on a colorful moving-platform."

While Lucia was practicing her performance, the surface began to heat up and flashes over the surface revealed strange symbols in the form of three-dimensional clocks. The surface then began to lose its firmness.

"Mester! What is happening I am sinking!" Shouted Lucia.

"Me too!" Responded Mester. His feet were sinking the way they do in the sand as waves come in.

A feeling of panic swept over them, the more they struggled the faster they sunk. The symbols kept spinning until they engaged in a position that made Mester and Lucia disappear.

"Oh God, no! What happened? Where did they go?" It took a second for Juan to realize they were gone. Terrified, he raced to get help, tripping over his own feet while trying to keep his balance. His screams were enough to awaken anyone on the island.

Mester and Lucia felt been caught in the vortex of a tornado, traveling at an unbelievable speed down a tunnel towards a light. Time had begun to dissolve into itself. Gravity pushed them in all different directions, until they crushed into nothingness. It was now beginning to feel warm. Finally, they found themselves in another dimension. It was like stepping into a vacuum, there was nothing tangible. The ethereal body with which they had traveled through the tunnel in seemed to be no more.

Lucia felt as if she had fallen into a deep sleep. *If I am in heaven, then I am at least next to Mester,* she thought.

They arrived to a glow in a space that was too white to be daylight. From there, each of their thoughts expressed as ultraviolet lightning, cutting in crazy zigzags toward the walls of the globe. It was similar to standing in the middle of a thunderstorm.

The Creator of the Universe

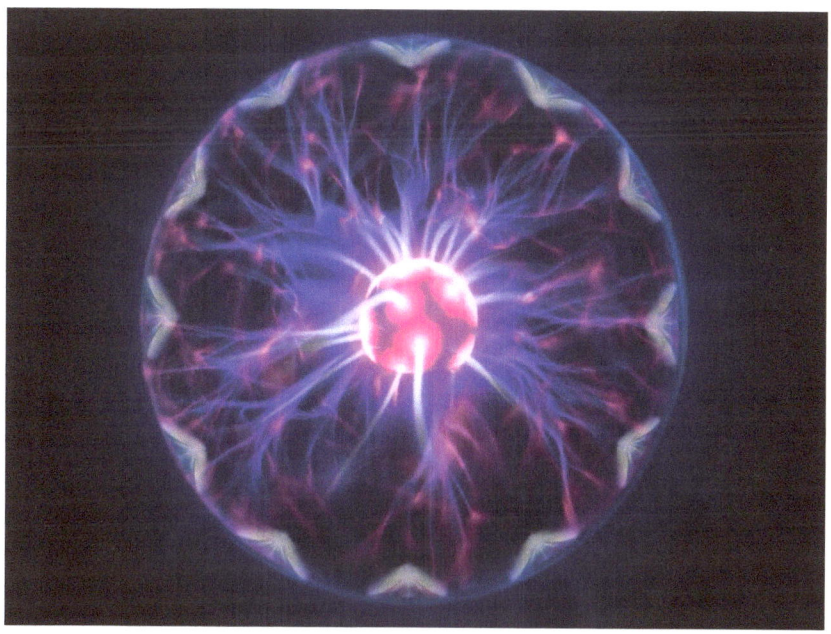

Mester and Lucia turned around, and through blurred vision, they managed see twelve beautiful crystal-niches surrounding them in a position of a twelve-hour clock. Each niche shined like shards of glass in different colors, holding what resembled a human figure inside. These beings were approximately ten feet tall, surrounded by a halo or glow of light. Their wings came in many sizes and colors. Their outfits were flowy, with long, draping sleeves that appeared to be an extension of softness and grace.

"Heaven is more beautiful than I could have ever imagined!" This time Lucia had no doubt she was dead.

One of the creatures laughed at Lucia's thought. It was small with grand ears and had on a golden cape more brilliant than his wings. With a beautiful harmony and without pronouncing a single word he expressed, "Welcome Mester and Lucia. We have been waiting for you. My name is Krausel, epitome of Muza, and I belong to the creation of Kozma."

"How do you know about Kozma? Where are we?" Unlike Lucia, Mester was very well aware that this was not heaven.

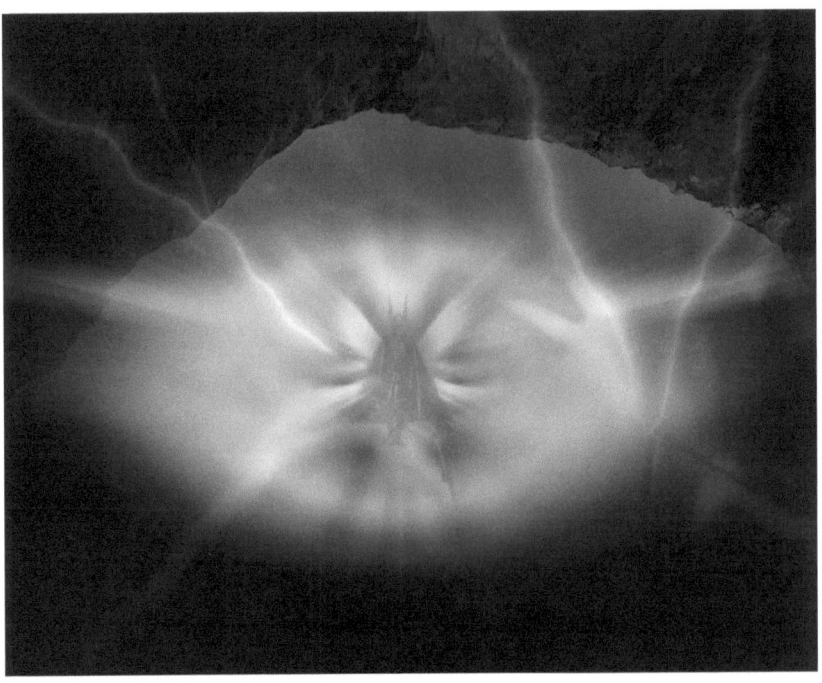

"Mester, we are well aware of your origin, as well as of your great mission here on Tellus. When your classmate, YinYang, created this hologram with the *to do* energy, you intersected it with the *to be* energy. This created a rotating nucleus hidden by the reality of Tellus. In this nucleus, is where we now find ourselves."

Lucia did not understand a single word, but at least she felt a certain degree of relief of knowing she was alive.

"Who are you?" Mester asked. "And how do you know all of this?"

"We are the twelve Epitome Angels of the creations, and our wings are inter-dimensional, allowing us to enter any dimension or vibration.

Lucia felt completely disoriented. She wanted to ask Mester a million things, but every time she tried to speak, rays of energy took their place. Her thoughts were heard like an echo in the middle of the conversation between Mester and the Epitome Angels. She felt her naked, her every thought was now exposed. She looked like a child when interrupting a conversation among adults. "Excuse me, I do not wish to interrupt, but how do I stop thinking? This is complicated."

The Epitome Angels enjoyed Lucia's spontaneity, especially Krausel and Musel, the Epitome Angels of Kozma. They had a very juvenile sense of humor and catching them at a moment they were not laughing was rare.

Krausel raised his shimmering wings and gave Lucia a sense of the divine spark. "You will now feel better. I gave you a little help or else you would have electrocuted the place with so many thoughts." Krausel and Musel's joyful laughter echoed through the place, cheering everyone up.

Mester needed to clarify several things, "I am sorry, but the more I think about it, I don't recall seeing any of you during the process of creation."

"Do you remember when the Creator gave each of the Gods two spheres to form your creations? There were twelve in total."

"Of course."

"Well, every one of these spheres had the mark of the Creator encoded within them, and that mark is us, The Epitome Angels. That is why there are twelve of us, one for each sphere."

"How were we never aware of you?"

"When YinYang altered the equilibrium, we were transferred due to the universal law of love for Tellus in hopes of repairing the damage. Even now, only you and Lucia are aware of our existence. We are unknown even to the Creator himself. The core of Tellus' hologram does not allow for us to be perceived."

"Why do you remain hidden in here?" Mester asked surprised.

We have a plan. If it succeeds, we will be able to free Tellus from this dimension very quickly. However, we cannot allow the intervention of the gods because they simply cannot understand this given reality unless they are here. You did come to us for a reason."

Mester nodded, and with a tone of enthusiasm, asked, "So, what is the plan?"

"We will show you. My name is Razquiel and my partner is Alequiel, Epitome Angels of Argyris. We belong to the creation of Losna." Razquiel had on a golden long dress that undulated slightly, matching Alequiel's suit. They followed similar patterns to that of their creator. Their prominent stomachs showed a half moon, which they carried with great pride.

Pleasant memories crossed Mester's mind, feeling himself drift off in his thoughts for a while before coming to a stop.

"A pregnant man?" Once again, Lucia's thought had escaped.

Razquiel and Alequiel looked at her so sweetly that for a moment their stomachs escaped from her vision of sight. A warm breeze enveloped her, shifting her inner world into a higher vibration. It was so pure that it allowed her to see beyond her physical mind.

The two Epitome Angels hugged each other so profoundly that their half-moons united into one full moon, projecting images. "Look closely, Mester, at how the two inverted pyramids—or Merkaba, as you have called them—spin in opposite directions from one another, achieving balance. This is good, and the Telluranians can obtain calmer, healthier lifestyles and maybe after some time and effort, can move onto the fourth dimension. But we have found a way to accelerate their learning process, allowing them to enter the fourth dimension quicker."

"What way?" Mester asked eagerly.

"The Angel Canal!" answered Razquiel. "Once a person is conscious of the use of the Merkaba and asks us for help, a canal of light is opened through magnetic fields emanated from here, creating a wider connection toward the fourth dimension. This propels the velocity of each individual's Merkaba, helping each person accelerate his or her learning process. However, for this to work, each person must ask for it. We cannot intervene if they do not ask us to."

The Creator of the Universe

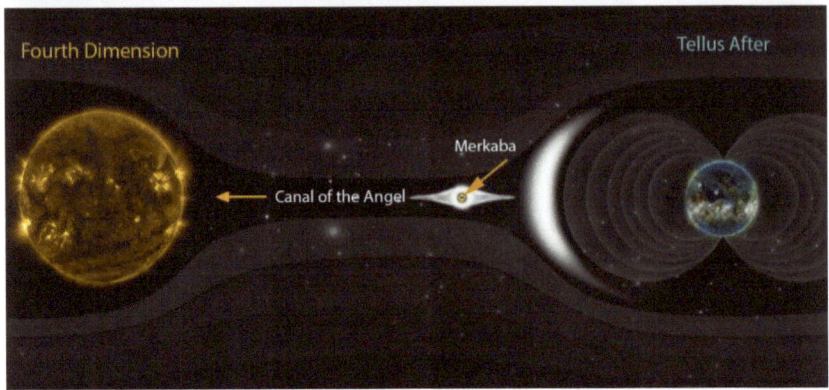

Mester could not believe it. It took a second or two for the new information to sink it. He felt a great worry lifted from his shoulders. He realized that he was no longer alone on his journey to help the Telluranians.

"How can I help?" Mester asked. "There are twelve of us, including myself."

"In this place, you will find everything you need. You will be able to create any geometrical figure you wish to help the Telluranians awaken their consciences. We are located perfectly within Tellus for you to use your skill. Since we are at the center of the magnetic field, the distance between your thoughts and their manifestation is zero here. Seeing as you are both here, your creations will be instantaneous, the way it was with the Creator, remember?" questioned Razquiel.

Mester's emotions expanded while envisioning his memories next to the Creator. "Ahemm…" Mester cleared his throat as he changed the subject, "But how are we supposed to carry all the geometric figures that we create here?"

"Twelve years in Tallen represents only twelve days in Moorea. Once you have finished, we will make sure to place your creations around Tellus."

At that moment, Mester remembered. "Excuse my impudence, but there is no food in Moorea and my friends must be starving." Mester said, imagining the great worry they must be under, especially Juan.

"Don't worry. They will all be brought here. However, they must enter in pairs of one man and one woman, opposing forces, because The Great Rainbow Sun only recognizes polarity. Just as you both found your way here, your followers must also follow the signs."

All the pieces were coming together. Clearly was not a coincidence that six women and six men decided to join him on the journey.

Within seconds, a blinding light heralded the arrival of Juan and Cayenna. Juan neared Mester to hug him but he could not, for he had no body. "Mester, I have been looking for you all over the island, but where are we? Don't tell me we are…?" His thoughts flashed across in nervous waves.

"Calm down, Juan. This is only temporary. The best part about this place is that we no longer need anything physical." Lucia was trying to cheer him up.

Mester greeted him with warm thoughts, letting him know the feeling was mutual. He was not simply a good friend, he had become part of his soul.

One hour later, equivalent to thirty days in Tallen, the rest of the group showed up. The Epitome Angels gave them a warm welcome, treating them as a precious gift of the Creator's light.

The Creator of the Universe

As if ready to start a ceremony, the Epitome Angels positioned themselves in their respective niches. In a coordinated manner, they threw a golden dust into the air. Unlike snow, gravity had no way to make it fall. The pixie dust swirled in the air above, pushed by the flap of their wings, while changing its colors with their level of consciousness. This opened the door to instant creations.

Mester felt himself regaining his abilities. Thoughts began emerging from him, taking shape of his deeper self. It was as if an artist had released his brush, embodying different emotions into dimensional figures.

Staring had become the only form of expression. The group was in shock. Each figure was so complex that they simply could not understand it in the third dimension.

Suddenly, all the empty stares from the rest made him react. "I am sorry I got a little carried away..."

"Mester, how in the world will we be able to do something like that? I can't even form a straight line." Thomas was scared of looking foolish, especially in front of a crowd.

"Do not worry Thomas. All you have to do is maintain your thoughts at an elevated state of consciousness. Connect yourselves to the unconditional love of the Creator. Only then will you be able to manifest your creations."

"But how? Is this magic?"

"No, this is the true process of creation across the entire universe. We are all artists in our own way."

"Apart from the spheres, can we also create pyramids like the Merkaba?" Juan asked.

"Yes, you can create any figure you like. What is important is that you comprehend the infinite number of possibilities as well as their significance. For example, the sphere has the highest vibration seeing as how all combinations derived from it, a major one being the Flower of Life, with a very high level of evolution. As the geometric shape shies away from the sphere, its level of vibration decreases and therefore, the level of understanding is limited."

"What can we do to help Telluranians evolve?" Lucia was determined to escape this mess.

"To reach unity, you must find integration. You have always seen duality as something normal: black and white, good and bad. If I had to explain the fourth dimension to you with mathematics, it would be with radial matrices and integers. Unlike the third dimension, or Tellus, in which the numbers are irrational or broken, they are divided."

"I can't escape mathematics no matter what dimension I find myself in!" Thomas' thought came off as a joke and even the epitomes could not help but laugh.

"Thomas, I understand your frustration, but trust that what you find so complicated in this dimension will not be so in the next. In the fourth dimension your geometric understanding, which you call mathematics, is innate. It will be as easy as breathing in Tellus."

The epitomes jumped in to clear up any confusion. "In this nucleus, you will experience something similar to what the fourth dimension would be like. In Tellus, you have three axes: length, width and height (x, y, z). The difference between this dimension and the fourth is an extra coordinate: time. This means that the time of manifestation is immediate. This will allow you to bring your creations to life much faster. This is the reason why Mester has been able to create these figures, an opportunity that is waiting for you as well.

If in the fourth dimension, we can materialize our thoughts, what could the other dimensions be like? Cayenna was attempting to understand something beyond her limits.

Mester made use of geometry to help his classmates understand the vastness of the universe. "There are fifteen dimensions before reaching *Unity* or *The Sacred Sphere*.

These dimensions are then located within seven different levels. I will explain to you every level so that you understand the responsibility that comes with creation."

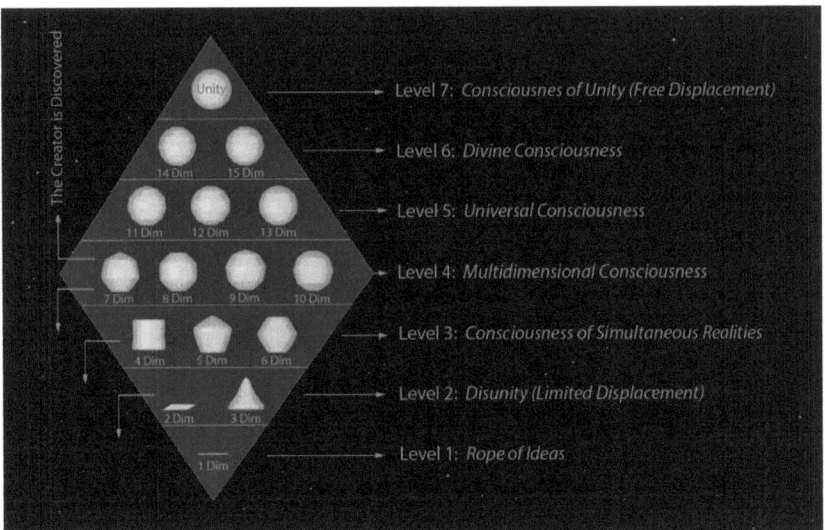

Level 1, Rope of Ideas. It is composed of the first dimension, which consists of lines or open strings. They represent the beginning or the sketch of an idea; nothing is concrete.

Level 2, Disunity. It includes the second and third dimensions. Here, the string closes to form membranes and three-dimensional figures. After a long time and a lot of effort, these ideas begin to take shape and become concrete. The vibratory frequencies are very low at this level, which is why creations here serve more individualistic purposes, which creates a separation from the whole and causes a delay in evolution.

Level 3, Consciousness of Simultaneous Realities. It is composed of the fourth, fifth, and sixth dimensions. Manifestations of matter and energy are instantaneous, due to higher vibrational frequencies. It is like living simultaneous and parallel lives, something like being skinny and bulky at the same time. Here, all manifestations are beneficial to the community, but not to the universe as a whole.

Level 4, Multidimensional Consciousness. It includes the seventh, eighth, ninth, and tenth dimensions. Here, is understood the infinite number of parallel universes. Here lies the capacity to express and feel the unity of the cosmos and all the beings that enclose it. It involves seeing everything that the universe has to offer, seeing all living things and realizing that we are looking at another version of ourselves. We are all the same. It is at this level when the Creator is discovered, and for the first time, they are allowed to see all the other dimensions placed at the higher levels. All unknowns become clear and the wisdom of the Master comes into play.

Level 5, Universal Consciousness. It is composed of the eleventh, twelfth, and thirteenth dimensions. Here, they take responsibility for the universe. The law of the divine plan of love is not only understood but also enforced.

Level 6, Divine Consciousness. The fourteenth and fifteenth dimensions form it. The relationship with the Creator is direct. Reparation actions are implemented to restore the Divine Plan.

Level 7, Consciousness of Unity or Sacred Geometry. It belongs to the sphere. Complete unity is finally achieved. It is the comprehension of the universe, where all dimensions become one, being one with everything. Pure consciousness is the ultimate essence of the universe; therefore, the power of creation is intrinsic."

"From the first day I saw you, I knew you were different from the rest... so much wisdom in one person..." Juan stated with great pride.

"My dear Juan, your thoughts flatter me, but you are just as capable as I am. There is no greater joy for me than to

The Creator of the Universe

see you all discover the power within you. One day soon you and the rest will master these concepts."

"Why do so many dimensions exist?" asked Eloisa.

"To prevent a creation of low consciousness from interfering with the more elevated ones."

"But if the sphere is the ideal dimension, why don't we just stay there instead of having to go through all the other levels?" Eloisa's question made Mester think about another reality.

"You all now have the capacity to understand something that changed the fate of Tellus. One of the gods named YinYang created this world that you call home, or what you will come to realize: duality. You all remember nothing because there is a great magnet of forgetfulness placed in Tellus to prevent you from remembering who you really are. The Creator has not stopped worrying about you all for one second. In fact, he wishes more than anything that this had never happened. That is why I came here: to explain to you all that however unfair this situation may seem, there is a way out and you are not alone."

Like a puzzle, the pieces were starting to come together. Things were finally starting to make sense to them.

"You did all of this for us? Came all the way here..." They now understood the great sacrifice Mester had made for them.

"Does this mean that you're... a God?" Lucia narrowed her eyes, scrutinizing her source.

Mester's stare accompanied by a crinkly smile was the confirmation she had been waiting for.

Lucia felt great admiration for Mester, but now he seemed forbidden to her.

"That means that you do not need us to make any creations here, right?" Thomas was trying to find any possible way out of the responsibility that lay before him.

The Creator of the Universe

"Thomas, come here. You will see that creating is not as complicated as you may think. First, you will have to imagine an open rope, and then close it."

"That is all?"

"Yes, just the way your thoughts express themselves through rhythmic vibrations; these will be perceived through the ropes, giving origin to infinite geometric possibilities. The form that your creation takes will depend on your state of consciousness and connection to the whole."

Thomas did not quite understand what he meant by 'state of consciousness.' With some hesitation, he imagined a vibrating oscillating string in a celestial color. Slowly, the undulating movements of the rope began increasing, until taking the shape of a twisted earthworm, due to his nerves.

Anticipating what was to come, Krausel and Musel raised their wings leading the melody of a beautiful lullaby, and with a tempo so sweet that it could have put an entire army to sleep. Thomas' nerves dissipated and a sudden sense of peace overwhelmed him. His once insecure hands were now firm, along with his thoughts. The waves of the rope lessened, now moving with great harmony.

Following Mester's instructions, he carefully connected both ends of the rope, forming a two-dimensional surface. In that moment, only one thought from Thomas was necessary to determine the final dimensional figure. As if the shape of a deflated latex balloon depended upon the level of consciousness of each breath used to fill it, he thought, *I wish to be one with the Creator*.

To everyone's surprise, this thought had created the highest level of the dimensions, the sacred sphere.

"How is this possible? How could I have created something like this?" Thomas looked at the sphere, overwhelmed with excitement, but filled with so many questions. "It can't be that simple!" He turned to the epitomes in search of answers.

The Creator of the Universe

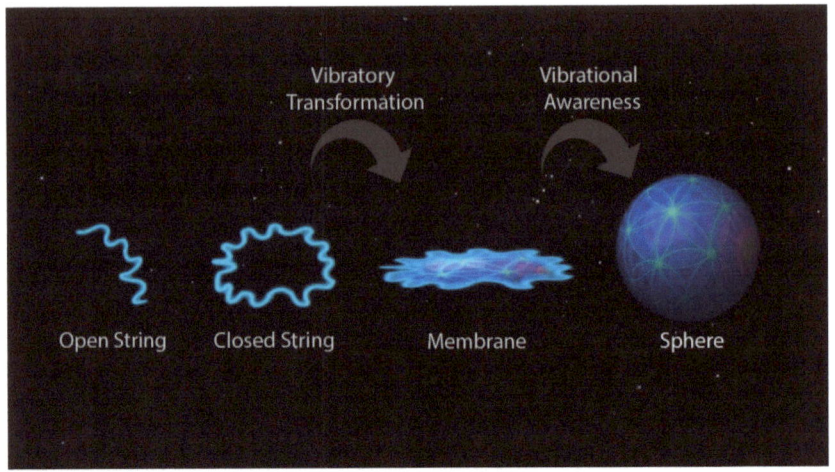

"All we did was emit a vibration to unblock all your doubts and fears. That was all." Krausel assured him.

The applause from the wings of the epitomes along with the praise from Mester and his classmates brought a new Thomas to life, one who was sure of himself, one that was not perfect, but was no longer scared of making a mistake.

"Well done Thomas. That is how simple the process of creation is. Starting a creation with a thought of love is the key element to success." Mester clarified.

"So then what happened with Tellus? Why are we so different?" None of this made any sense to Dr. Geo.

"You are not different. You are just in the process of learning. The creation of Tellus was originated from the tetrahedron and it is our responsibility to return Tellus to the origin of the sphere."

"But how will we do that?" Dr. Geo questioned. Everything that was occurring defied his beliefs, and there were still a few more to come.

"All you have to do is show the Telluranians the figures that we create here. They have an intrinsic genetic code of love within them. Just the simple observation of these figures will awaken a vague memory in them. The truth existed before lies, just like love came before hate."

"Just like we came before the creation of Tellus," Geniel and Ganel, the epitomes of YinYang's creation interrupted. They could not hide the sadness in their eyes, but their smiles showed they still had hope.

"What other figures can be created apart from the ones you have already made?" Juan's mind was limited.

"Infinite others, as infinite as your imagination. Do not be scared. Feel free to create in a universe with no boundaries. I will give you an example. This is the seed of life. Its geometry consists of seven spheres of the same diameter. They overlap in such a way that the center of each circle finds itself in the circumference of the six other spheres. And so you can add more spheres in different positions and angles, creating even more complex figures."

Juan's focus seemed to be on only one figure, the Merkaba. He had been living in a shadow until one trip in it changed his life. It planted a seed of hope in him, something he thought had been lost forever.

With the perfect conducive environment, ideal collaborators, conscious thoughts, serendipity, and even spiritual muses, they came up with unique creations, producing stunning artistic works. Their fears began to dissipate, liberating the spirit of creation. It was as they had forgotten how to stand still due to their newfound lust for creation.

The Epitome Angels watched them curiously from their stone niches. Since the Epitome Angels had no control over their innate instincts, they could not help but intervene ever so slightly upon the creations. Their emotions blended with the group in the most delicious of ways. Krausel and Musel, from Kozma's creation, made the spheres move harmoniously, placing them at precise points of intersection. Razquiel and Alequiel, from the creation of Losna, created a force of attraction between the creations, grouping them together into unique patterns. Amael and Michael from the creation of Astra, gave life to the spheres, reproducing them at great speed. Raphael and Fabiel, from the creation of Celare, offered a palette of infinite colors. With the gifts of motion, attraction, quantity and pigment from the epitomes, they produced intriguing figures.

However, not everyone intervened. Geniel and Ganel, from the creation of YinYang, as well as Bramel and Aniel, from the creation of Brahman/Mester, found it prudent not to intervene in order to prevent an imbalance.

The Epitome Angels did not lose sight of the creations, especially those of Mester. His comprehensive knowledge and skill of geometry were beyond their imagination.

The hours passed quickly, never giving a single thought to the time they spent creating in the nucleus, until a slight flutter behind broke their concentration. Amael flew next to them. She was a walking masterpiece; her blue hair was flowing endlessly, framing two emerald stone eyes. Her

The Creator of the Universe

cheekbones were high and prominent, giving her a confident look. "Excellent job. It is now time to awaken the conscience of the Telluranians." She expressed in a sweet way as the pixie dust progressively disappeared.

Proudly observing the creations, they wished they could exist in that moment forever.

The epitomes had taken great pride in how much everyone had evolved. In addition, having Mester among them had been a great privilege.

"Where can we find our creations once we return to Tallen?" After all that work, Juan had grown much attached to them.

"They will be placed around Tellus: in temples, cathedrals, mosques, museums, and a few other places. Once you return to Tallen, it will not take long for you to discover their locations because of the reactions they will cause among the people. These figures will awaken superior levels of consciousness among the observer by sending sensory stimulations in a subliminal way. Just remember that once you have returned, even though you are no longer on Moorea, we will continue to work together. With the Merkaba, the Angel Canal, and the Sacred Geometries you have created, we have a greater chance of awakening."

Unexpectedly, multiple golden balls of light in different sizes grouped together around the creations. These Spirit Orbs grabbed all the figures and flew out into the surface of Tellus like silent messengers, blending into the darkness of night to avoid any chaos.

There was a silence in their souls, happiness and melancholy lingered in the air. The empty space signaled the end of their deliberate efforts and the beginning of new hope.

The Epitome Angels rose with wide-open wings simultaneously nodding in reverence. "We have nothing else to say, but thank you for all your help, and may the power of love from the Creator guide you always."

In the blink of an eye, their magical surroundings disappeared.

"Where are we?" asked Isabel.

"If I am not wrong we are back to where we started." Dr. Geo's neurons went back to play.

"I must say, even though we are back on the same Great Rainbow Sun, we are not where we started, we are much further." Juan stated.

Mester gave him a big smile.

"From up here, it is like looking down at the world," Lucia was trying the raise everyone's spirit, "we can see beautiful glass trees, noisy waterfalls, the sea, and..." she stopped.

"The sharks," Dr. Geo finished for her.

"Perhaps twelve years have been enough to restore King Aldon's cavalry, or maybe even double it," Eloin thought aloud.

"It's a good thing we're no longer in the nucleus with the Epitome Angels. Otherwise, your thoughts would have become reality..." Alline called to his attention.

With a sweet voice, Mester added, "Now that you have seen what our thoughts are capable of, you must be very careful of what you think. Even though in the nucleus, your thoughts of creation were direct, it does not mean that your thoughts do not affect creation out here. It still does, but significantly slower."

"Now that I think about it, how come nothing bad or sad ever happens in the nucleus? It was all harmony and beauty and now that we're back, these thoughts of worry have crept back into my mind." This concerned Juan due to his prior experience with the powerful effect of negative thoughts.

"This is due to polarity. Negative ones attack your good thoughts. It is in that duality that you are at risk of

The Creator of the Universe

losing the battle unless you maintain your positive thoughts."

"But how do you achieve those consistent positive thoughts?" asked Juan who was now shrugging.

"By simply remembering your good experiences as soon as the bad ones appear. That way, the negative ones lose strength. Notice how you all thought about King Aldon. Why don't you think about how fortunate we were to have crossed the canal when we did? On the other hand, think about how we brought just enough food with us to maybe last us a week, and ended up not eating anything for twelve years? The list goes on."

Eloin's tiny eyes widened. He looked down and noticed that his belly had practically disappeared. He was ecstatic. "Humbleness aside, I can truthfully say this is the best shape I have ever been in my life!"

Among the explosion of laughter, Alline's nod of approval awakened an illusion in him he had long forgotten about. For the first time, he was receiving a flattering gesture by a woman that was not due to his culinary abilities.

"Look! The canal is opening!" Eloisa yelled in panic.

"But how? We didn't feel an earthquake..." said Dr. Geo remembering their prior experience. He stepped down from the Great Rainbow Sun platform to make sure. His body instantly felt like jelly, unable to talk from the continuous shaking, "Ittttt musttttt beeeee theeeee platfooooorrrrrmmmmmm...." His voice was following the vibrations of the Earth.

Mester finished his sentence, "Yes, the Great Rainbow Sun is suspended on the water. That is why we were unable to feel the earthquake."

"Another positive point to think about," uttered Juan.

"Very good Juan. That is what I like to hear."

When they saw Dr. Geo finally stop shaking, they stepped down to help him. His glasses were slanted as if his ears had different heights and his body was spinning without direction.

Without another word, Mester and Juan each wrapped Dr. Geo's arm over their shoulders and commenced their journey downhill. With gravity on their side, it was time to run. Among stumbles, they moved as fast as they could, fearing they would not make it in time.

Once on the shore, they saw the protagonists return to the scene. Hungry sharks were leaping through the air attempting to catch any pray they could. If they thought it had been difficult to cross the Dragon Belt before, now it was close to impossible.

The Creator of the Universe

11

The Creator Looses Patience

As if in a game of chess, there was no longer just one pawn, but twelve guarding Tellus. Mester had finally been able to share his knowledge with his peers.

This was not something that YinYang had seen coming. He tightened his hands into fists as his face reddened. YinYang's discomfort was so obvious that Kozma, incapable of resisting a spontaneous outburst, played a musical note: "Tara-Ta-Tan!"

There was a spark in their souls; finally everything was beginning to work. Nevertheless, deep down, they all had mixed feelings. They were happy because the sooner Brahman finished his mission, the higher the chances to be reunited. Even though they knew there was no guarantee that he would be able to escape the reality of Tellus without becoming trapped in its endless cycle. However, they were unaware of the epitomes or the Angel Canal.

"I bet my power of creation that Brahman will exit Tellus having completed his mission. I created him, and I know what he is capable of." The Creator nodded his head as a sign of certainty, the way a proud father would.

This was the last thing YinYang wanted to hear. "First, you wish to destroy my creation, and now you play favorites?

The Creator of the Universe

I thought we were all equally important to the Creator," YinYang protested, fully aware of his intention to manipulate.

The Gods could not accept such a lack of consciousness. Their eyes simultaneously turned to the Creator, waiting for his reaction.

Fires of fury gleamed in the million narrowed eyes of the Creator, while he weighed the pros and cons of the decision he was about to make. If he could go back in time, he would have never repeated his creation leading to YinYang. "From now on, I remove your ability to hear, prohibiting you from interfering with the hopes of the Telluranians—and ours as well."

The gods were surprised by the Creator's decision, even though deep down they were celebrating, especially Losna, who unconsciously let a soft smile slip.

YinYang fell into an eternal silence. He was locked inside his evil world, separated from the delight of creation. YinYang interpreted the Creator's decision to limit him as a punishment. With this one act, the Creator had opened the door to resentment in YinYang's heart, and his ignorance did not allow him to understand why his father could not tolerate his way of being. That was his role after all: to tolerate, or so he thought.

Mester and his disciples were ready to cross the Belt of the Dragon. Losna exerted her force to maintain the water level low, but the enraged sharks added a whole other level of difficulty to the journey.

Astra moved next to Losna and sent a message:

"Kommos and Kamusis all around
Come to Moorea to show your songs
For an hour keep the sharks away
As Brahman and his friends find their way"

The song of the Kamusis was so heavenly that the sharks became lost in a trance, while the waves emitted by the Kommos disoriented them.

Astra and Losna felt like they had done well together. However, one small detail was out of their control.

12

The Return to Tallen

A concert of divine voices surrounded the island, making the sharks grow strangely calm. The Kamusis and Kommos arrived as close as the water level would allow. Despite their distance, it was not enough to stop the powerful voices from reaching their eardrums.

"Do you hear that? What a beautiful song. Its excellence, perfection, superiority... it's so relaaaxinggg..." Juan was in a half-conscious state, in between sleeping and walking, while drooling on his chest.

Isabel and the rest of the women's faces evoked admiration at the beauty of such a song. On the other hand, the men seemed speechless. Eriseo and Eloin had forgotten to blink, while Thomas, Dr. Geo, and Juan had the silly smile of someone in love.

"What is happening Mester? Look at Juan and everyone else! What is wrong with them?" Eloisa waved her hands in their faces to try to get a reaction, but it was useless, their abilities to function voluntarily were suspended.

Mester immediately recognized the voices. He could not help but laugh at the sight of Juan under these conditions.

"Do you know what is happening, Mester?" asked Lucia.

"Yes, it's the Kamusis and Kommos and they are here to help us. Their interdimensional song crosses all borders, which is why you see our friends in that state. They are capable of showing you all the beauty in the universe with just one song. It is almost too much to take in, so I do not blame them.

"Now, the question becomes: how do we cross with them standing, but asleep at the same time?" Lucia had the sweetest chuckle.

"In this state they are highly receptive to directions so every one of you grab hold to the partner with which you entered Moorea with and gently guide them to Alekos, they will do whatever you command." Mester explained.

Now the roles had reversed, it was the girls who were in charge of the men's' well-being. "How the times have changed," Isabel giggled.

The sharks swam about, no longer providing a threat. The coral continued to be an obstacle, but by not having King Aldon's cavalry after them and the sharks looking for their next meal, they were able to better focus and arrive to the shore without a single cut this time.

Finally they arrived to Alekos. Night fell and the waters returned to their normal levels. Now, the Kommos and Kamusis were able to get closer to the shore. With great pride, the Kamusis were swimming in a very seductive manner, sporting their stylized body of golden scales along with the Kommos, slapping about their powerful tale, sounding almost like a gunshot.

"I have never seen such a captivating feminine figure before…" Alline had always considered herself attractive, but this was another kind of beauty. It was transcendent, almost unreachable.

The Creator of the Universe

Raising themselves up by their tales, the Kamusis and Kommos gave a sign of reverence toward Mester, swimming away in a series of high-speed leaps until disappearing.

Soon enough their songs were no more. Juan began to come out of his trance. He stretched as if waking up from a long dream. "Ahhh, how did we get here so quickly when just a moment ago we were on the other side?" He said, scratching his head.

"Do not worry, Juan. What is important is that we're here now," Mester did not want to embarrass him.

The other men heard Juan, asking themselves the same question. Dr. Geo instead focused on his watch, which marked eleven o'clock at night, and it was now dark out. At last, everything was back to normal.

Now the only noise heard were the ocean waves striking the shore. They anxiously and repeatedly searched their surroundings, checking for signs of danger that would not come.

"It's not a full moon yet!" Dr. Geo pointed up at the moon. "There is still one day left before the full moon appears.

"The ocean has now opened a day earlier for us." Mester thanked the heavens, or better said, the Gods.

They moved toward the mountain of Alekos with slow and heavy steps. The Cliffhangers were no longer there. They took a deep breath, preparing themselves for the journey up.

"I have to admit, even though the Cliffhangers were very irritating, I wish they could be here, for going all the way to the top would have been easier with them." Dr. Geo dropped with a gasp as pain slammed through his knees.

"Ready? Three...Two...One...Go!" With a long drop, one of the Cliffhangers fell straight down in their direction. Right before hitting the sand, it grabbed Mester by the waist raising him up.

The Creator of the Universe

"Surprise! Guess what? Mother Rock heard of your success and let us grow before time to welcome you all and celebrate!"

With what seemed like little effort, the vines took ahold of everyone and passed them around, rejoicing their great accomplishment.

The entire group reached the top enjoying this moment of bliss. Everything up until this moment had been perfectly coordinated, and of course, there was no escape from the Cliffhangers for other tales.

> "One day an old man decided to share half his profits
> He thought he was very good for it
> Not knowing that this was just the beginning
> A vast universe was ready to show
> Being good was only the first step
> You must give it all in the great universal staircase"

They looked to one another trying to decipher the riddle presented before them.

One phrase specifically caught Mester's attention, *give it all...*

"What do they mean to tell us with that?" Dr. Geo asked hesitantly.

The Cliffhangers became agitated, and instead of explaining, they told another story:

> "Explanations are lost,
> It is only the tale that counts
> Your interpretations will fly
> Based on your wisdom it will apply"

Dr. Geo frowned with his eyebrows. Those were the type of vague responses that threw him off base.

"It is clear that everyone can interpret things as they wish. There is no way for the Cliffhangers to be precise, due to the fact that the universe gives you room for free will," Mester clarified.

After all the excitement, the sleepy flowers began to close from exhaustion. The Cliffhangers barely managed to say goodbye whispering in a dreamy voice:

"Walk while there is light
Do not let the darkness surprise you"

"Light? It's nighttime!" Dr. Geo interpreted everything far too literally.

There was importance to every phrase that the Cliffhangers uttered. They never just talked for the sake of talking. Hidden between their messages was great wisdom.

With no baggage this time, their walk back should have been easier, but the repeating phrases within their heads seemed to be weighing them down.

They had advanced maybe fifty feet when they heard a voice yell, "Mester, son!" The voice erupted from between two bushes a few feet ahead.

With his heart pounding, he saw someone familiar. The old woman had a grey- white hair. Her back was slightly hunched and she had the resigned look of one who knows that at her age life has stopped giving and only takes away.

It took a few seconds before Mester could react. He ran into his mother's arms, hugging her so hard as if he was trying to make up for his twelve-year absence. He could see that these years had taken a toll on her, but in his heart, everything was as it had been.

"Where is my Father?"

Hazar could not meet Mester's eyes.

"Mother, what happened?"

The Creator of the Universe

"After you left for Moorea, the king was infuriated at having lost the majority of his troops, especially Sivilion. His fury was so great that he came to our home in search of your father and took him to the dungeon. He told the public that if you were as powerful as they said you were, you would have no problem rescuing him. Tomorrow marks your father's twelfth year in his cell."

Mester swallowed hard, unable to speak. He fell to his knees. He did not dare imagine how much his father must have suffered all these years while he was away, even though for him it had only been twelve days.

"I will fix this. You and Father will grow old together." Mester was determined to erase that look of sorrow off his mother's face.

"What do you have in mind Mester?"

Let's go mother. I will explain later. We cannot lose any more time. Mester hugged her to provide her with some support, for she seemed much weaker, and with each movement there was the creak of old bones.

Descending the mountain was the least of Mester's concerns. Imagining all the hardships that his father must have endured over the years was torturous. In need of some kind of sign, he looked up to the sky. A full, 'honey moon' was high in the sky.

"Do you see that?" Cayenna pointed.

A smile stole across their faces before they could stop it. There was a quick flicker of lights, softly buzzing through the dark skies. Oddly enough, the lights were forming a path in the opposite manner they were walking.

"Look! Fireflies! I have never seen so many. It must be another sign," Juan interrupted.

Mester wished to have not received that sign right at that moment when the only destination he could keep in mind was getting to his father. He stuttered for a moment and took a deep breath, "Let's follow the fireflies."

Together, the fireflies created a path of light in the air with curves and spirals, clearly marking the direction they should follow.

They quickly came to a halt.

"Wow! Look at that. It looks like paradise!"

In the distance, the darkness was dotted with small glimmers of light, making it look like an enchanted place. The glow of the fireflies mesmerized them. Amid the green of the forest was the reflective white strip of a waterfall. This beautiful place, in addition to the sensation of the gentle drizzle from the waterfall, was just what Mester and Hazar needed, a moment of relief.

"Ohhh this is perfect, a place to wash my toes in!" Excitedly, Cayenna took her shoes off, her feet felt swollen and fiery, but just when she was ready to jump into the water a noise made her freeze.

Boooommm! Stingrays that looked like gelatin crystals were swimming below the waterfall. They jumped and turned ever so graciously. With every jolt, they emitted an electric current that not only illuminated their surroundings, but also caused a portion of the waterfall to run out of water.

"Did you see that?" Isabel squealed.

"Of course I saw that, it almost killed me!" Said Cayenna with static in her hair.

No! I was talking about the waterfall, there is something behind it, but I can't be sure", Isabel said.

They curiously waited for the next discharge. After a few seconds, a brilliant shock of white came, revealing more clearly this time some sort of entrance behind the waterfall.

"Let's go! What are you all waiting for?" yelled Juan, he was ready for the treasure hunt.

Juan saw a path fade behind mist and small bushes. It was damp and very slippery, so he held onto a stone wall along the way for support.

"Ouchhh!" That wall is burning," Juan screamed with a deep pain within his hand.

Eloisa tore off a piece of her skirt and tied it around Juan's hand. His skin was red and warm, but her sweet touch was the best ointment available.

Dr. Geo came after him. He moved his hand close to the wall until he sensed the intense heat. "This wall is at least eight hundred degrees. But how? It's not lava, it's not fire…"

With dilated pupils, they all scanned around for any explanation to this phenomenon.

"Look over there! If I am not wrong, the wall has a carving on it, but I need some light to read it." Lucia said.

As if her words were an order, hundreds of fireflies came closer, eating away at the darkness for a while.

"Yes! It is a message," Lucia clarified, excitedly: *At the end of the road, there is always a final test. Show what you have learned. Step into the water and walk to the cave.*

"Walk to the cave? That is a guaranteed walk to our deaths." Raising one brow in an expression of doubt, Dr. Geo took the message as a joke.

They stood there, unable to speak. Somehow, despite these crazy words, their intuition told them otherwise.

Juan thought for a moment and approached the border of the lake, ready to go in.

"Wait Juan! What are you doing? This is absurd!" Dr. Geo warned him.

"Don't you see? Our faith has been called into action. After twelve years of lessons, what else could this message be referring to?" Juan questioned.

Mester smiled. He knew Juan was pure of heart, but now he was strong of spirit and brave. That look of unassailable confidence in Juan's eye said he could do it.

More sure than ever before, Juan moved his right foot forward. As if ready for a fall, he released his weight. He waited for gravity to hit, but it never did. Looking down, his

The Creator of the Universe

eyes were trying to make sense of what he saw. Suspended just millimeters over the water, the stingrays were swimming bellow him, it was almost like having a glass floor beneath his feet.

Everyone's mind focused on Juan's gentle footsteps, bewildered as they saw him successfully crossing over the water. It looked like a stunt.

The blood drained from Dr. Geo's face.

Juan kept walking. Every step was more confident than the previous one. He reached the front of the cascade, and with a deep breath, he crossed the wall of water, disappearing behind it.

Not sure on what to do, the group looked at Mester. "You all just saw a grand act of faith, we just have to follow him. The path is now open."

Everyone except for Dr. Geo followed Juan. It took him a few extra minutes to let go of his logic and take a leap of faith.

When they entered the cave the last thing they expected to find was so much illumination. Thousands of fireflies were covering the walls, glittering like stars in the sky. On the ground, spreading like weeds, were hundreds of 'Manjar Mushrooms,' ironically, they King Aldon's favorite due to their rarity.

Eloin was salivating at the thought of it. He pulled as many mushrooms from the ground as he could and washed each one in the waterfall. Eloin was very meticulous when it came to food. With great hurry, he picked up the traces of firewood on the ground and built a bonfire.

"I think someone is about to regain those lost pounds," Alline said with the intention of telling him to control himself.

"Uhmm…It's for all of us," he said, winking.

They sat as close as possible around the bonfire to feel the radiating warmth. The smell of the savory mushroom in the fire prepared by Juan and the light effect that the fire had among the walls of the cave created a cozy atmosphere, one that even Mester and Hazar could enjoy.

With their stomachs full, Mester took advantage of the moment. He felt that there was a reason behind this interruption on their way to Tallen. "Starting tomorrow, we must go our separate ways to guarantee the expansion of wisdom here in Tellus."

Mester stood up and moved towards one of the walls in the cave. The fireflies moved aside to give him space. He took a piece of rock and drew Tellus divided into twelve parts, assigning one to each person. He then also added several sacred geometric figures so they would be fresh in their heads. He also sketched for them what the Epitome Angels of Losna had shown him and Lucia, how the Angel Canal had been opened to facilitate the journey to the fourth dimension. Mester tried to give them as much information as possible, considering that Hazar had not been with them in Moorea.

"What I am about to ask you is perhaps too much, so feel free to say no. The best way for our message to spread correctly is for us to distribute ourselves evenly along Tellus. Every one of you will have the responsibility of discovering the sacred geometric figures that we created to expand our wisdom among your assigned area. You must do this carefully. This information is very delicate and could cause chaos if is not communicated correctly. Begin by teaching about love and helping your neighbor, but more importantly, practice what you preach. That is how you will gain followers. I will take responsibility for Tallen and its surroundings."

All they could hear was the falling water as the others exchanged doubtful glances with one another.

"What if something happens to you?" Juan broke the silence.

The Creator of the Universe

If King Aldon attempts to end my life, he will be doing me a favor."

Hazar raised her hands to cover her ears. She could not handle the thought of losing her son.

Mester looked at them, "When others see that I have offered my life to show them the way, they will truly believe."

"Believe in what?" his mother asked, not understanding.

"In unconditional love. Even though on Tellus love is not perceived in its original form, you will see in me the true meaning. You will see someone who is incapable of hurting another in self-defense. You will see something beautiful, and you will ask yourselves if that is what awaits you. This hope will connect you to the love's source of our Creator."

"But once they see and understand this, how can they use it to enter the fourth dimension?" Juan asked.

"This will increase their faith dramatically and will help them balance their Merkaba. In addition, if they seek help through the Angel Canal, their souls will evolve, allowing them to enter the fourth dimension. It is a space much more similar to that of the Creator's. There are no physical items, which in reality, aren't needed."

"What do they eat there?" asked Eloin with the juice of the mushroom still running down his beard.

"Souls are only energy and feed off their environment. The fourth dimension is like a beautiful meadow that emits a radiant light that is perceived by the auras, while nourishing their souls at the same time."

"Like the nucleus of Moorea?"

"Yes, when we were in the nucleus, we were in the infinite dimension of the sphere, where time does not exist. Just like the Epitome Angels, we fed off energy."

"If all dimensions have a problem, like Tellus having a loss of wisdom, what is the problem in the fourth dimension?"

"After Tellus, everything is very different. This is similar to how a baby first crawls and a year later begins to walk and continues to walk for the rest of his life. Once you leave Tellus, you will continue to walk with love for the rest of your journey. For now, only focus on learning and evolving enough to leave your current dimension."

"What happens if we don't do it correctly? The Creator, as you call him, will he be angry with us?" Alline asked.

"Of course not! Our Creator would never be angry with any of you for such a thing. It is quite the opposite actually. All he truly wants is for you to succeed with your best possible efforts to reach ascension from this place. Rather than focusing on whether or not the Creator will be upset with you, you should focus on escaping this world to a better one."

"I definitely won't be living the same life upon my return. Well, if I return," Alline said, fully intending to move to the next level. "Everyone will see such a great change in me that they will believe just by taking one look at me."

All the prostitutes held hands and nodded at each other. This served as yet another reason why the prostitutes had joined them. There was no better example of beings who had risen above from pure love. Everything became clearer, including Mester's responsibility to his fellow Telluranians.

"I wish to trade places with you," Juan said suddenly, looking at Mester. "I will take watch over Tallen. I am not concerned about something happening to me. All I care about is that you remain safe." His eyes watered as he practically begged Mester.

"The mission here on Tallen is much more complicated than you can imagine, Juan. When they come after you, you will be well aware that anything you say could lead you to harm's way, and in self-defense, you will lie when death is staring you in the face. This will send Telluranians the wrong message. However, if they see someone stand firm in telling the truth of love without caring about the consequences, it will open the door to the other world. Until now, no single person in the history of Tellus has not acted in self-defense when faced with conflict, which is why, when they witness someone acting in a different manner, a great veil will fall, and you will continue with your mission. All people need are instructions on how to use the Merkaba along with the Angel Canal."

"As you wish, Mester." Juan swallowed.

"What do you say if between all of us we use the Angel Canal, right now?" asked Mester.

They jumped in excitement, including Hazar, who did not understand very much. Holding hands, they followed Mester. "From the balance of our Merkaba, we ask the angels of the epitome for help. Through their wisdom, our thoughts become clear, our knowledge is heightened, and our genuine desires are quickly manifested with the power of love."

Hazar felt a great peace overwhelm her and could feel the familial ties among all of them, something she had not perceived before they had left for Moorea. She knew they must have lived through something beautiful. Finally, exhaustion took hold of them, and the fireflies made sure to watch over their long sleep.

The following day, daylight broke through the waterfall. Their eyes searched for the fire that had kept them warm throughout the night. It was gone. An absolute silence overtook the cavern. Their eyes transmitted what no one wanted to say: goodbye.

The rainy day seemed to match their emotions perfectly. This time Dr. Geo guided them towards Tallen, leaving behind the drawings on the wall, which little they knew, would be used for their later mission in Tellus.

"Look, Mester," Dr. Geo kneeled down to get a closer look. "Horse tracks and a lot of them if I may say. They are

The Creator of the Universe

fresh. I would say they passed through here no more than four hours ago. It must be the king's cavalry and they are headed towards the Alekos Mountains."

"Of course, they think we will be arriving tonight during the full moon," Juan clarified.

They swallowed hard. The sign had become clear. "If the fireflies had not deviated us from our original plan, we would have definitely run into the kings men. They not only would have taken me prisoner, but all of you as well, along with any hope for Tellus."

Even though Hazar did not know as much as the rest, she could not help but notice how perfectly coordinated things were around Mester. She was clear on the fact that there was a divine plan at hand, except for Domino's twelve years in prison.

They continued along, this time much more alert. They traveled via shortcuts through the shadow of the trees, perfectly hidden until they reached Tallen.

"Very well, the time has come." Mester cleared his throat, "I have no words to thank you all for what you have done for me, and especially Tellus. May the Creator bless you and guide you and may love follow you always." Unable to mask the hurt, tears escaped. This was the first time they had witnessed Mester in a vulnerable state.

These words pulled the group into a hurricane of emotions.

Lucia was the first one to jump in Mester's direction. She squeezed him so tightly that she very well may have been suffocating him. She wished to have stayed with him, but she knew he would always be with her in her heart.

The screaming sobs from Juan interrupted them. Something inside him was whispering this could be the last time he would be standing before Mester.

Mester was worried about Juan faltering on his mission, so he stayed firm. "Juan, I believed in you from the very beginning, and you have proven me right. That strength is within you, not in me. I simply showed you the way. I will be present in every word and thought that you teach. That is how I will always live on."

Juan breathed deeply, his words helped cheer him up. Continuing his teachings was the least he could do for Mester.

Each member of the group carried a knot of pain in their chests, unable to form words. Their eyes said everything they felt, and their goodbye hugs were never ending, filled with beautiful memories.

Some were worried about getting lost since they were unfamiliar with the geography of Tellus.

"I have never even left Tallen, except for Moorea of course," Alline said in a quiet voice.

"Do not worry Mester. I will make sure that everyone arrives to their given destinations safely. You can count on that," Dr. Geo assured him.

With his arm around Hazar's shoulders, Mester kept his gaze firmly on the others as they moved farther away. Every two steps, Juan turned around to look back at Mester, his expression giving him every reason to think that he would soon start walking in reverse. Mester lifted his hand, letting him know everything would be okay. He watched them walk through the meadow until they disappeared from his sight.

Despite knowing they would be all right, he could not help but think about all the challenges they would face. In that moment, he decided to seek the Angel Canal. "My dear Epitome Angels, I ask for your guidance and protection over the others, that their thoughts be clear and their hearts act as shields of love. May you protect them."

Hazar could feel his pain. She hugged him tighter and, in an attempt to lift his spirits, said, "Perhaps you'll be able to see your father."

This statement brought Mester back to reality. "We will go directly to King Aldon. He has a debt to settle with me, not my father."

"No! That is not what I meant to say! We should go ask about your father since they have not let me see him."

Mester hugged her and set off at a quick pace. They took a longer route to avoid having to cut across the city and risk being seen. The palace was almost deserted. They did not see a single guard on duty as the king had sent every soldier to look for him.

A short guard was standing at the entrance of the palace, covered in a light armor, too big for his frame. Since all the guards had left in search of Mester, this was his only opportunity to pretend to be a knight. He was whistling a low tune to himself when he suddenly stopped.

"Mester, what are you doing here?" He immediately recognized him. "You weren't supposed to arrive until tonight…"

"I wish to see the king." Mester requested.

Surprised, Toppon told him to follow him. "He will be quite excited to see you—more excited I would say than your own father," he said sarcastically as he tried to keep a normal pace.

His words made Hazar tremble.

King Aldon was in a private healing session with the magicians of Maldar, Bolingdor, and Bezadel. He had been suffering for twelve years from grave headaches and insomnia. His eyes were like those of a raccoon, and his expression was not much different from that of a corpse.

The doors to the salon opened with great force, hitting the guards standing on either side. "My king!" Toppon yelled. "Look what I bring you."

There was nothing the king hated more than being interrupted during his healing sessions. He was lying with his face toward the ceiling and eyes covered in bandages soaked in dream honey, a potion prepared by the magicians to alleviate his aches and make him sleep.

The king ripped off the bandages, ready to send Toppon to the dungeon for his impertinence. However, his breath seized when he focused on only one face — Mester's. The solution to all his problems was finally standing before him.

Jumping up, the king's ego returned with vengeance. He clenched his hands into fists, trying to control himself. He half smiled, arching his eyebrows, making it completely apparent how many terrible ideas were crossing his mind.

"So, you finally come to ask for my forgiveness for your lies and what you did to my troops?"

"No, I actually come to ask that you liberate my father. He has nothing to do with my wisdom."

"Wisdom? Wisdom about what, Mester? The only thing you do is create geometric figures and label them as spaceships. I don't know about the rest, but I personally don't buy it."

"You don't have to believe it if you don't wish to. It's simply free will."

"Free will is what I will be using on you for trying to be Mr. Wise Guy. The only one who gives orders around here is I. The only one who sets the rules is I. The only one who decides if you live or die is I. If your God is so great, then let him come save you." The king was like a ticking time bomb. "Answer me one question. Why did you go to Moorea? What did you do for all those years?"

Mester could not lie, but he also would not give a thorough answer. "To learn about the true meaning of unconditional love."

"Twelve years to learn just that? I can learn that in one day. Do not lie to me. What are you keeping from me?" King Aldon was insistent, convinced that something had been planned against him.

The Creator of the Universe

"Unconditional love can take a whole lifetime to learn here on Tellus."

"What are you referring to, Mester?" King Aldon was beginning to lose his patience.

"If we were to practice unconditional love between you and me, you would first release my father. He has done nothing. Second, you would allow me to continue with my teachings, since this makes me happy and it brings no harm to you. You should actually be happy for me, just as I am for you that you live in such a beautiful home with many luxuries, which I hope make you happy."

This had taken a different turn than expected. King Aldon felt as if he was losing control of the conversation. "Listen closely, Mester. Just to show you that I do, in fact, understand unconditional love, I will liberate your father, but in turn, you will take his place for having made your father suffer twelve years for your impertinence."

Hazar cried out, "But it's not Mester's fault, it's–"

Mester stopped her. "Mother, everything is fine. This is exactly what I need him to do. Everything is going according to plan." Hazar's mind was in chaos, but she kept quiet.

"Bring me Domino!" King Aldon yelled.

A few minutes later two doors creaked open to allow a skeletal, bearded man to walk in, accompanied by two guards. Behind the patches of dirt on the man's skin was a familiar smile, but it was his eyes that gave him away, they were undeniably Domino's.

"Father!" yelled Mester, as he and Hazar ran to him.

"What are you doing here, Mester? You should not have come."

"Silence! You at least have a son who cares about you, even if he is crazy. You are free to leave now. Mester will take your place. I can't promise that he'll survive as long as you did, especially if he doesn't learn to keep his mouth shut,

The Creator of the Universe

something I see he has a problem doing." King Aldon laughed sarcastically. He made a gesture to the guards, who immediately secured Mester's hands with chains. "Take him to the dungeon immediately and make sure to make him feel at home."

"Nooooo! Please! Do not do this to my son, take me!" Hazar could not tolerate any more pain.

"Ma'am, I believe it is better that you leave, or would you prefer to join him?" King Aldon was taking far too much pleasure in this.

Mester looked at Domino and moved his head slightly to the side, urging them to leave.

With mixed feelings, Domino hugged Hazar as he led her out. Hazar felt her bones break from the pain.

Mester's cell was a hollow cube of concrete stone. No windows. Nothing else to stare at other than the bleak walls. There was no light, no shadows, no furniture, just the sound heard through the tiny cracks on the wall from the torture room. He felt trapped in his own thoughts, but with hope in his heart.

After Sivilion and Natzuel had disappeared, Gazu had become the Commander. He was a tall man with a hoarse voice. His unwavering glare showed his relentless personality. There was only one thing he seemed to be scared of, and that was King Aldon.

The following morning, Gazu heard news that he was sure would put the king on edge.

"Your Highness, excuse my interruption, but... I am not sure how to tell you this. I learned from a reliable source that a spaceship of great size has landed in Machelpekira."

A cup encrusted with diamonds fell from the king's hands. "What are you talking about?" he narrowed his eyes. "Corroborate this information first and then interrupt me!"

"You're Majesty, that's exactly what I did. I sent troops to investigate and it is..."

"It is what?"

"It is true, Your Majesty." His abnormally muscular legs seemed to have gone weak.

King Aldon did not think it had anything to do with Mester, seeing as he was locked up, but his intuition told him otherwise. "Bring him to me. We will all go see this place together. Let's see what new story he comes up with this time."

"Bring who?"

"What do you mean 'who'? What is wrong with you? Mester! Who else?" With each yell, the king grew closer to him, wanting to rip this man to shreds.

"Immediately!" Gazu was highly strung. A few seconds later, he brought Mester in the room and threw him before the king's feet.

King Aldon was breathing deeply, carefully choosing his words. "Mester, how do you continue to be a problem even when you're locked away?"

"I am sorry, but I do not know what you're referring to," Mester replied, confused by his question.

"Oh, you don't know? Let's see if that's true. Gazu prepare my troops. We will be going to Machelpekira."

The king grew anxious. The journey was not a pleasant one; the carriage was jolting every other second from the speed they were going at. When they arrived at Machelpekira, the roads were congested, and they clearly were not the only ones heading in that direction.

"Move aside!" Yelled Gazu, "The king is coming through!"

From the carriage, they could hear many voices shouting, "King Aldon has finally met his match. Whoever did this is far more powerful than him!"

This comment pushed him over the edge. The king's face reddened from anger as his eyes turned to Mester. He

The Creator of the Universe

just needed proof he was behind this to make him disappear once and for all.

The spaceship was in the middle of the desert, a great length away. The air was thick and hazy. The horses were pulling the king's carriage across the desert, but the wheels were sinking deeper and deeper into the sand, making the horses' efforts useless.

When they reached the highest ridge in the sand, hardly daring to believe it, there was a pyramid of about five hundred feet in height, made up of huge red stones. Based on the technology at the time, it would have been impossible to build something like this, especially in less than a day.

"Who could have made something like this?" Gazu exclaimed.

The Creator of the Universe

The pyramid was familiar to Mester, but he did not remember seeing any of them create this figure in Moorea.

Kind Aldon's head was spinning. This was too much to take in. "Tell me you had nothing to do with this," he spat at Mester. "Is this another one of your 'works of art'?"

"Excuse me, Mister Aldon."

"King! I'm the king!"

Mester continued. "I am not sure. No pyramid was created in Moorea, only a Merkaba, unless...."

"Unless what?"

"Unless this isn't a pyramid. The Merkaba could have been embedded through the planet of Tellus and therefore this is just one its vertices. If this is so, then there should be more figures like this one throughout Tellus."

This had turned into a living nightmare. It was like a virus that spread uncontrollably.

The Creator of the Universe

"So if I may ask, how did you manage to carry this tiny little figure with you?" the king asked, clearly making fun of Mester.

"I did not bring it with me."

"Then who did? Mester, just give me answers once and for all!"

"The spirit orbs brought them."

King Aldon was clenching his jaw so tightly that he felt his teeth were about to crack.

"And who are these orbs?"

"They're the messengers of Moorea."

"I don't know if this is the truth or not Mester, but don't you think enough is enough?" The king's jaw did not loosen. His fists tightened, as he grew closer to the enormous blocks of stone. Each stone was perfectly carved. No human being could have done this. He felt a sense of solemnity. Under no circumstance did he wanted for anyone to feel what he perceived standing so close to the pyramid. It was more powerful than his entire empire.

"Keep everyone away from here! If they wish to see it, they can see it from a distance. From now on, only myself and those authorized by me can come near it." If he could have built a wall around it, he would have.

Despite all his restrictions, he could not stop the crowd from gathering in awe at this masterpiece. Trying to hide it was like hiding the truth. It was bound to come out sooner or later.

Face to face with Mester, the king whispered, "Listen to me closely Mester. For your sake, I hope you're wrong about this." His face turned from one of fury to one of ruthlessness.

"Gazu!"

"Yes, Your Majesty."

"Listen carefully. I want you to send Martel with half of my troops to investigate if there are any more of these "things" around Tellus. At the same time, I want my archeologists to dig the base of the pyramid to see how deep it is. I don't care how long it takes, but start immediately!"

The news spread like wildfire.

When Hazar and Domino arrived, they tried to reach Mester. Despite the pushes from the crowd, they finally managed to reach the barriers established by the king. The sign in front read, "No trespassing. Private property of King Aldon."

Even though they were not allowed to be anywhere near Mester, they could at least see him from afar. He was significantly thinner, but radiated with happiness. "Domino am I imagining things or is Mester smiling?"

"Mmmm…" Domino could not see well from far. He turned around and saw a familiar round face with a spyglass on one eye.

"Look! It's Bruce!" Domino ran as fast as he could toward him.

Bruce was in shock, he almost did not recognize him. "Domino, is that you?"

"Yes, it's me. But skinnier." Domino smiled. "Please, Bruce, I need to borrow your spyglasses. I need to see Mester."

"I just saw him and, as a matter of fact, Mester looks joyful. See for yourself."

"No, Hazar. You are not imagining anything. I know that look of our son. Something good is happening. Nothing would make him happier than saving this planet, from what I have understood at least."

After waving their hands and arms for several minutes, they were finally able to catch Mester's attention. His smile widened as he nodded, letting them know that everything was under control.

Ten hours had passed since their arrival in Machelpekira. The king had his eyes on the clock, waiting for his troops to return with news.

Meanwhile, the archaeologists had been tirelessly seeking any possible answer to such a strange phenomenon.

"My king!" yelled Trason, Tallen's most renowned archeologist. He had a long pointed mustache, which he constantly spun with his fingertips when he was deep in thought. "It turns out these rocks are made of solid minerals from natural origin, weighing several tons. What we cannot understand is how they got here. There is no sign of them being dragged. They seem to simply have been placed here."

"Trason, how can someone place something so heavy here without first dragging it?" The king managed a fake smile.

"I don't know, Your Majesty," his legs were trembling like the strings of a guitar.

At this point, King Aldon understood that Mester was something more than an imposter. He had powers, which was something the king could not allow. However, he still needed to obtain more information before making a decision.

"I see you weren't lying when you said the stones were placed by... those things. Tell me, why did they do it?" asked the king.

"To show everyone the reality of Tellus. Telluranians must learn that in order to ascend into the next dimension, your inverted tetrahedrons must be balanced. Only then can you reach the true origin of creation, or the sphere."

"How do you know all of this Mester? Who are you really? Go on, I'm listening."

"I am the Son of the Creator."

"Oh really? So then, tell me why insert a Merkaba in Tellus? Isn't it easier to simply draw it or build one like the one you did?"

Mester knew the epitomes were behind this. "It was probably to achieve a greater connection to the Angel Canal." He did not want to go into much detail of how many Epitome Angels there were.

The size and surface of the pyramid walls worked as an echo, expanding the sound. The whole conversation between Mester and the King could be heard all around, as if the multitude were only a few feet away from them.

"And what is this 'The Angel Canal' you speak of?"

"I have already explained to many of you the importance of balancing your Merkaba. But, we have obtained a new tool." Now, Mester spoke louder to make sure everyone could listen. "Asking the Epitome Angels for help will manifest your wishes in a more immediate manner."

"So, if I ask your angels for you to disappear, you will?" King Aldon gritted his teeth.

"They are not my angels. They are everyone's. Plus, they only help when it's a petition derived from love."

"Enough! Gazu, take him to... to his throne." The king said slyly.

"Umm... I am sorry Your Majesty, but where is this throne exactly?" Gazu asked, completely lost.

"Where else! The top of the pyramid you idiot! From there he will able to prove just how powerful his beloved angels are." said King Aldon, directing a sarcastic glance toward Mester.

Brilliant rays hit from above. It was as hot as any beach without the benefit of a cooling breeze. The path was challenging.

From below, they all witnessed how they treated Mester. His nearly shredded up tunic revealed his sunburnt skin as his feet were skinned alive with no shoes to ease his climb. Between climbing and laughing, the soldiers took water from their canteens, only offering it to Mester when it was already empty.

Mester's strength, however, was so great that it guided his steps. Even without water, Mester remained ahead of them.

It was almost midnight when they finally reached the top of the pyramid. From above, a sense of omnipresence dominated the area. The floor was filled with hundreds of foreign inscriptions and right where they were standing was a drawing of a sun with twelve rays of light surrounding it.

"Look... an altar for the Creator's Son," Gazu said with a smirk. "Enjoy it while you can." They bent over with laughter.

"Bring him down! It's too hot and he must be starving!" yelled the people. The crowd was so desperate that the king ordered extra security to make sure no one dared to interfere.

For three days, Mester could not have looked more peaceful. He felt as if he were back in Moorea with thousands of mushroom eyes watching him. In fact, he preferred this place to the dungeon. Only three thoughts crossed his mind: that his parents remain safe, that his teachings multiply, and that he returns to the Creator's side.

At noon on the third day, Mester looked up to the sky, the radiating sun penetrated his mind, making him realize something. He looked at the writings on the ground. At the top of the circle it read, "Here are the twelve angels," and at the bottom it read, "Be it done according to your will."

Of course! The Merkaba expands the strength of the epitomes. They surround me. He focused on each ray, and each one had another one similar to it, just the way there were two epitomes per creation. *Be it done according to your will? It means I can materialize my dreams right now.* He bent forward to stand up, he was weak and his legs were shaking. Closing his eyes, he envisioned a beautiful golden

The Creator of the Universe

Merkaba, ready to take him home to be reunite with the Creator. He remained in this state of concentration for an hour, but he felt that the density of Tellus prevented his manifestation, even when the Epitome Angels were doing the most they could.

Meanwhile, among the crowd below, a voice caught everyone's attention. "My king! My king!" Martel had clearly returned with some news. "It is true. We were able to confirm the appearance of two more pyramids just like this one, and there are rumors of more."

"Enough. Kill him!" yelled King Aldon with zero hesitation.

Despite the shouts from the king and his soldiers, absolutely nothing could be heard from the top of the pyramid. Their words were carried away by the wind.

The crowd could hear exactly what was happening though. Hazar felt her heart stop. She may not have understood much about the Angel Canal, but with much courage, she took Domino's hand falling to her knees. "My dear Epitome Angels, take my son between your wings, and take him quickly away to that world of love from which he came." She no longer felt the need to keep him with her. She only wished for his safety and happiness.

Bruce and the people around listened to her repeating these words over and over. They did not understand much of what she was saying, but it was the intensity of the pray that caught their attention. They shared her words until Hazar's desire spread through the crowd. Soon, thousands of people were praying from the bottom of their hearts for Mester.

The intensity from the vibrations of love radiating from the hearts of so many people was so great, that it surpassed the expectations of the Epitome Angels. This unexpected phenomenon not only manifested Mester's wishes, but it also broke Tellus' nucleus in half, liberating an even greater level of the Epitomes Angel's power of manifestation.

Mester's body was becoming ethereal. The sunlight now was passing through his body, losing his physical presence.

As a final act, a beautiful Merkaba appeared around him spinning with great force. It reminded him of the same bright light that had brought him to Tellus. He felt a force lifting him up, the ground floor where he stood was getting smaller and smaller as he traveled away from it. The distance between Mester and the surface of Tellus continued to grow, and soon, he lost sight of everyone.

Mester disappeared before the eyes of the crowd, like some grandiose magician's trick.

Hibakujumoku! Yelled the natives of Machelpekira, falling on their knees with arms up, recognizing the miracle."

The Creator of the Universe

The burning hard stare of the king was fixated upwards, deeming this phenomenon as impossible.

Hazar sighed, a feeling of relief overwhelming her soul. It was unexplainable, as if she knew for a fact that her son was now safe. "Son, wherever you may have gone, thank you for picking me to be your mother. I do not know what you came to learn from me, but I learned everything from you. You have filled my heart with love, and I will continue to spread your teachings because I know that we will soon be reunited."

Domino tried to make sense of all the confusion around him. He fell to his knees before Hazar. "He's gone... our son is gone." He looked up at Hazar in the hopes of some reassurance.

"He is all right, Domino. Do not worry." For the first time, Hazar was handling the situation better than he was.

From the Merkaba, Mester could hear his parents. In that moment a beautiful butterfly with an extraordinary range of patterns and colors landed on Hazar's shoulder.

"You see, I told you, Mester is fine, otherwise how do you explain this beautiful butterfly making its way all the way here, flying though the desert with such a strong wind. Our son is fine now." Hazar's voice showed no doubt.

Hazar and Domino hugged with relief and happiness; until the King's chaotic yelling interrupted the moment.

"What are you waiting for, Martel? Get up there, and find out where he went! It's just another one of his tricks." King Aldon could not bear to think about the possibility of Mester disappearing, undermining his unsatisfied pleasure of torturing him. He still had not bestowed enough pain upon Mester to repay him for his twelve years of agony.

When Domino saw the fury of the king, he covertly took Hazar by the arm, and with a few pushes, made their way out of the crowd. "What are you doing, Domino? Why are you in such a hurry?"

"Have you not realized it yet, Hazar? Once the king sees that Mester is, in fact, gone, he is going to take it out on someone, and that someone will be us. It's not that we must run away out of fear, but we must go help spread the knowledge Mester left us with."

The thought of her husband being incarcerated yet again gave her the necessary adrenalin to run. Without another word, Hazar grabbed Domino's arm leading him out of Machelpekira.

Just as they had suspected, King Aldon did not delay in searching for them, but it was too late. Hazar and Domino had packed up their things and disappeared without a trace.

The neighbors gossiped among themselves about what had happened that day. They brought to life several different versions of the story. The only thing that held true was that the eleven disciples, plus Hazar and Domino, continued with Mester's teachings. They made sure to leave written legacies in every language, along with thousands of images, which Mester had left in his diary. Although they did not understand all of them, they knew that at some point in time Telluranians would.

As time went on, Mester's legacy lived on in every corner of Tellus. Souls evolved faster with the help of the Merkaba, the Angel Canal, Sacred Geometries, and now the rupture in the nucleus. Since then, many generous souls have moved on to the much-deserved fourth dimension.

13

The Welcoming of Brahman

The gods did not lose sight of Brahman for one second. They stood around Tellus, awaiting the results from his great departure.

YinYang observed every detail, and although he could not hear, he could read the happiness across each one of his classmates' faces. He knew something had gone wrong—at least for him.

Then, with the force of a comet, a bright white light grew closer.

"Is that him?" asked Kozma.

It has to be him! The Creator thought.

Within a few seconds, a golden Merkaba appeared before them. Its velocity decreased as their anxiety heightened.

"Yes! It's Brahman!" Kozma jumped up and down, playing trumpets of victory all around them. Celare painted a magnificent garden using every color possible. The waterfalls emitting from Astra's hair splashed onto him, showing her excitement.

With no hesitation this time, Losna's force of attraction was so strong that it generated a magnetic movement in the form of a whirlwind. The Gods had to try as hard as possible not to let themselves be dragged by it, except for Brahman, who had no problem being drawn into her this time; their eyes, their lips, and their spirit all melted together at once.

The rest of the gods then surrounded him, while Kozma leaped over, taking Brahman by surprise. "I knew it! I knew you would return. You have always been my fav–uh, well, would you like to hear what I composed for your welcoming home?" He hoped no one had realized his sudden change of topic. He did not want to hurt anyone's feelings.

With great pride, Kozma stood before Brahman. "I composed a song for you a long time ago, a symphony that can mend any broken heart, and I named it, "The Universal Victory of Love."

The music mended their broken hearts, like a wave covering up any cracks in the sand. The song spoke to all of them, except for YinYang, who could sense his defeat.

Only Our Love
Verse

In the universe were we live
We share the same life
Flows like the waters
Shine like our light

Accept it within you
Fall from hate
Be the light of today
Understand our faith.

Chorus

Only our love will live
Only our love will save us

The Creator did not know what to do with all the excitement. For the first time, he felt something strange.

After having observed the Telluranians and their emotions for so long, he felt the need to cry.

Brahman moved towards the Creator. He flashed back to their last goodbye, and the pain he had felt, now dissolved. They placed both arms around each other with a strong squeeze, invoking deep feelings of warmth and safety. Unexpectedly, they both felt an instant transfer of energy between them. The Creator felt something strange for a moment, but his excitement did not let him dwell on it for too long.

The Gods immediately noticed the change in Brahman. Now, Brahman and the Creator were equal in size. *How is that possible?* They thought.

This moment was the checkmate move of the game for YinYang. He felt he had failed in acquiring the Creator's attention, just as he had failed within his own creation. From the side of his eye, he observed every one of Brahman's movements, angered by his sudden growth spurt. *Ugh... as if one Creator around here was not enough...*

Now Brahman could perceive things that before would have been impossible. He now had the capacity to create spheres of light just like the Creator. It could practically be said that they were one in the same now.

The Creator was still confused. "I don't exactly understand what happened, but I am happy it happened to you," as he thought about the dangers of someone else having gained those powers...

"My Creator, I do not plan to make use of my powers unless you authorize me to do so. I did not do this intentionally. If there is any way to return these powers, I will do so immediately."

"Oh no, my dear Brahman! Take them as a gift for your great labor. You have earned them. If there is someone who will make good use of them, it is you. Of that, I have no doubt."

The Creator of the Universe

Between all the excitement and joy, it was impossible not to feel YinYang's darting stares. He produced an unexplainable discomfort within the group.

They all caught up with one another, and Brahman explained his experiences and perceptions from Tellus, which were not necessarily what the gods had interpreted. Among other things, he explained to them the existence of the Epitome Angels; an advantage YinYang did not know existed.

The Creator did not take his eyes off YinYang. He was isolated, like always, and with his head titled downward, the Creator thought for a moment that he was repenting his actions. "Now that Brahman is back with us, I return your ability to hear, YinYang." The Creator looked at him, hoping he had learned his lesson.

Seeing there was no way out, YinYang turned to manipulation. "My Creator, thank you and I give you my most sincere apologies for all the trouble I have caused. I was very irresponsible and I let my desire to win blind me. Is there any way I can make it up to you?"

"YinYang, I just hope that you have learned from your mistakes." He was still not convinced of his sincerity.

"If only you could give me another chance, or two spheres, I promise to do better."

"Better than what, YinYang?"

"Well, it's something that will make you happy," he replied, not wanting to give too many explanations.

"What would make me happy is for you to behave differently with your classmates. That you would be loving for once…"

"But how do you want my dark side to be loving if it is dark. That is how you created me my Creator. I didn't choose to be like this."

In that moment, the Creator felt a great weight of responsibility land on his shoulders. *What could I have been thinking when I created YinYang? He was right. After all, he was my creation.*

Meanwhile, there was a consensus among the gods to try to find a solution to YinYang's problem.

"There must be a way to fix this mistake, my Creator. We will find a solution." Brahman tried to comfort him.

"I suggest we send YinYang to my creation, Argyris, the way Brahman went to Tellus, so he can learn about love," said Losna excitedly.

"I am not sure that will work. For once he returns, he will regain his same powers and abilities, just the way I did," explained Brahman.

"What would happen if the Creator transfers some of his powers, the way he did with you? That way, he may be able to break his equilibrium of polarity?" Kozma questioned.

"The problem is that he would have greater powers, and there would be no way to tell how much greater," the Creator clarified.

"How would we eliminate polarity?" Losna was deep in thought, searching for an answer she already seemed to have.

"But by eliminating polarity, we would eliminate YinYang?" Celare asked.

"Not necessarily, we would neutralize him. Let's see if with my powers of magnetism I can manage to alter his polarity, or maybe even invert his magnetic field."

"And how would you do that?" Astra asked somewhat confused.

With fixed eyes, she responded, "By inverting the balance on his head. Do I have your permission my Creator?"

The Creator nodded and she slowly moved towards YinYang.

With his gaze stuck on Losna, YinYang let a wry smile slip. *This is just what I needed, for them to try to change me too.*

With both hands over YinYang's balance, Losna created a rotational field over its axis. The balance had rotated about ninety degrees when YinYang's dividing line began to disappear, and his body became uniform.

"It's working!" Kozma announced.

YinYang's features became different. He no longer felt hate or love. Everything was numb. "What is happening to me? This is the same as being dead. Stop it!" With anger taking over, he clenched his hand into a fist and launched it at Losna's stomach.

Losna fell unconscious. Only the glimmer of a half-moon radiated from her stomach now. Brahman felt his lungs stop. He bolted toward her, cradling her in his arms. It was the first time he saw Losna so defenseless. In that moment, he grew so angry that he wished with every ounce of his being for YinYang to disappear from their lives, forgetting about his newly developed powers.

"Stop!" yelled the Creator.

However, it was too late. In that instant, YinYang had already disappeared.

"How? Where did he go? What happened?" No one understood.

"Oh no! It was me..." Brahman rested his head in his hands, trying to make sense of it. "I forgot about my new powers. What have I done? It is my fault. I made him disappear, didn't I?"

"Calm down Brahman, he is in some part of this Universe. As my creation, he cannot disappear, only transform." The Creator tried to console him.

"Does that mean I can bring him back if I wish for it?"

"Pretty please? Why don't we all just sing a song?" Kozma interrupted, trying to change the subject.

"It doesn't work like that. In that moment, when you thought about separation, a rupture was created that can only be fixed if YinYang wishes for it, for rejection is not part of love."

Brahman breathed in heavily, wishing he could take it all back.

"It is not your fault. I transferred powers to you before you were ready. The power of creation holds great responsibility, especially when things don't go according to plan." The Creator added, "I don't know which is better, to have YinYang close or far away. When he was close, I could at least know what he was up to. One thing is for sure, no matter where YinYang goes, my Epitome Angels of love will always be with him. He originated from them, after all. We may confront other difficulties down the road, but in the end, all will return to the origin of love." The Creator said in hopes of raising Brahman's spirits, as well as his own.

For the first time in a very long time, they were somewhat at peace, and even though they could not find YinYang, they never took their eyes off Tellus, lending a helping hand whenever possible. This creation was, and always will be the priority of the gods, until the day the unification of the universe is reestablished by the law of love.

www.ingramcontent.com/pod-product-compliance
Lightning Source LLC
Chambersburg PA
CBHW041432300426
44117CB00001B/5